C 19 ECONOMICS

BY ROBERT MILLER
Rainmaking
The Magic of Selling
Second Wind

BY HENRY PARK
Henry Park's Road to a Million

BY ROBERT MILLER AND HENRY PARK
Fading Dreams and Rising Fears
Latino Investors Entrepreneurs
& Advisors

C19 ECONOMICS

Your Guide to Personal

and Business Finance

ROBERT MILLER
HENRY PARK

ISBN 978-0-9975887-6-7

NEWPORT COAST CLUB

To Ali, Katie, Preston, Dylan, Audrey, Dominic, and all the world's children.

Oh, and there we were all in one place
A generation lost in space
With no time left to start again

— Don McLean
American Pie (1971)
Don McLean

PROLOGUE
HOW WE GOT HERE

The CCP has launched an orchestrated campaign, across all of its many tentacles in Chinese government and society, to exploit the openness of our institutions in order to destroy them. To secure a world of freedom and prosperity for our children and grandchildren, the free world will need its own version of the whole-of-society approach, in which the public and private sectors maintain their essential separation but work together collaboratively to resist domination and to win the contest for the commanding heights of the global economy. America has done that before and we rekindle our love and devotion for our country and each other. I am confident that we — the American people, the American government, and American business together — can do it again. Our freedom depends on it.

— William Barr
Attorney General of the United States
July 17, 2020

A prologue is used at the beginning of fiction books and is an opening to a story that establishes its context. Since this is a non-conventional nonfiction book, we are starting it with a prologue.

When President Richard Nixon visited China in 1972 few believed that China would become a serious competitor of the United States. That was a fatal error. We failed to understand — and continue to ignore — the philosophy and ambition of the CCP. After Chairman Mao Zedong's death in 1976, Deng Xiaoping — the "Architect of Modern China" — achieved an amazing series of market-economy reforms through his motto: "hide your strength and bide your time".

China has now made its big move to become the world's sole superpower. The invasion of the China virus has served as a catalyst to the most terrifying takeover that the United States has ever known as we struggle to fight off the CCP and the increasing threat of domestic terrorism. We will survive the deadly virus, but we may never entirely recover politically and economically from China's overt actions. PRC has thrown the first punch. This is when America puts on the gloves.

In pursuit of global domination China allowed the virus to infect the world and lied about it. Most Americans were naïve about China's long-term agenda and the world was caught off guard — ill prepared for the direct and collateral damages of the pandemic.

The virus hit the United States and the world like an invasion from outer space — creating a perfect storm for chaos. We fear for our lives and those of our friends and family members. Government agencies, local, state, and federal responded slowly and unsurely. There was little, if any, coordination, and whatever faith we had in our leaders quickly disappeared.

With one mistake after another fueled by misinformation and a lack of leadership the economy almost slowed to a halt. Businesses shut down or tried to remain open by adapting to the confusing and ever-changing regulations. With millions out of work and most people "sheltered in place" or "socially distanced" we became angry, frustrated, scared, and very anxious. Then a single event ignited our nation and started us down a suicidal path. We might have acted much differently under normal circumstances.

We have been emotionally torn apart — Democrats vs. Republicans, liberal vs. conservative, left vs. right, poor vs. rich, or often blacks vs. whites. And this is the time that we must fight for our lives and the survival of our economy and political system.

Someday the China virus will be under control. The demonstrators, rioters, and rabble-rousers will eventually settle down. Businesses and schools will open back up. People will go back to work. Our economy will recover. But the CCP will still be there.

The costs will be unbelievable. Loss of lives will be astronomical, and the financial burden will be in the trillions. Psychological damage will be deep and long-lasting and will include severe emotional complications and suicide.

All this because the People's Republic of China wants to become the world's superpower. Hopefully, after reading this book you will agree that we cannot let this happen. By the time you read the epilogue you will realize how real the Chinese threat is to America's present and future and exactly what you must do to take control of your personal wealth and secure your future.

Preface
Robert Miller

I'm dyin' for some action.
I'm tired of sittin' 'round here tryin' to write
this book.

— Bruce Springsteen
Dancing in the Dark (1984)
Bruce Springsteen

Legend has it that Pablo Escobar began his career as an entrepreneur by stealing gravestones and sanding them down before reselling them. From humble beginnings he became a billionaire who reportedly brought in approximately $420 million a week in revenue and controlled 80% of the global cocaine market. I wonder if "El Patron" ever read an economics book.

Although this is not an economics book — this may be the craziest, wackiest, and most eclectic book you have ever read. Enjoy!

PREFACE

Henry Park and I met at the Center Club Orange County in January of this year to talk about writing a financial guide. The next month the China virus turned the world upside down and we decided to focus our book on the effects of the pandemic including the economy and resulting challenges and opportunities.

I chose Henry as a coauthor because he knows how to make money. And because Henry cannot be accused of white privilege. He is a first generation Korean American whose story is one of rags-to-riches-to-rags-to-riches.

Five months after starting our book we are publishing *C19 Economics* which has morphed far beyond a financial guide to include the background information you need to understand how our nation's wealth is being devastated by the pandemic, China's obsession with destroying the United States, and the internal forces that are determined to dismantle our economy and democracy.

My first book, *Rainmaking*, was originally intended to be about sales but ended up being about making dreams come true.

A sales book followed — *The Magic of Selling.* Information extracted from both books is included herein.

Over the past several months our friends and associates have advised us to hurry up and publish our book before the pandemic ends. We were not concerned about their warnings because this book was never intended to be a pandemic survival guide.

Intentionally *C19 Economics* is raw and unplugged with no attention to book correctness — or political correctness.

This book was written for our own benefit to organize our thoughts and create strategies for building and protecting wealth. If we impact your life in the process that would be a welcome bonus.

I love America and it concerns me to know that our economy is being threatened by Communist China. After reading *C19 Economics* you will understand the threat and — more importantly — what we must do to protect and strengthen our economic system. It is not an exaggeration to say that our way of life depends on it.

The most imminent danger to our American way of life is not PRC but are the forces within America that call for the dismantling the U.S. economy and political system.

Politics were not intended to be included when we began authoring our book. Recognizing how the pandemic unfolded and the collateral damage to our economy and society it would be irresponsible not to address political issues.

We each have our own stories and our stories influence how we feel about America. How we feel about America determines our actions. Those actions include how we vote, what we do with our lives, how we express ourselves, and what we have to say. Henry shares his story at the end of the book.

My own story starts with William Wilcoxon who left London at age 34 with his 24-year-old wife Margaret and their 2-year old son John. The little family sailed on the good ship *Planter* and arrived in Boston on May 6, 1635 — only 15 years after the *Mayflower* dropped anchor off the coast of Cape Cod. So, you might understand why it hurts me deeply to see the cancel culture obsessed with destroying every shred of my family's twelve generations in America. Who gives them the right to judge those who gave their blood, sweat, and tears to make America great? They are domestic terrorists.

One of the things that makes America great is the First Amendment which guarantees the "freedom of speech" and "the right of the people to peacefully assemble" — the operative word being *peacefully*.

Anarchy has overtaken the streets of America and we must immediately quell the violent demonstrations and stop the murders. We can tolerate blood on Wall Street but not on Main street. We will never be able to mend America's economy unless we can mend America's hearts and minds.

May God bless America and protect you and yours. Henry and I have included our contact information at the back of our book and hope that we will hear from you.

— Robert Miller
Irvine, California
July 26, 2020

CONTENTS

Before You Begin

Don't bend; don't water it down; don't try to make it logical; don't edit your own soul according to the fashion. Rather, follow your most intense obsessions mercilessly.

— Franz Kafka

C19 Economics is an eclectic collection of words, thoughts, and dreams designed to inform, entertain, and inspire you — and help make you wealthy.

CHALLENGE

Invest an hour in yourself and make a list of what you expect from *C19 Economics.* Commit to immediately leverage what you learn and take advantage of emerging opportunities to build and protect great personal wealth.

_____

_____

_____

_____

_____

_____

This book may be the wackiest financial book that you have ever read. It is intended to be simple and easy to read —written in sixth grade English. It is filled with quotes, movie lines, and song lyrics. Just when you think you are beginning to understand it then you probably are not.

There are underlying messages on the pages of *C19 Economics* — that the American economy is strong and resilient — and that there are virtually unlimited emerging opportunities for you to actively participate in America's economic renaissance as an **Innovator, Investor, Entrepreneur** or **Advisor.**

The best way to maximize the benefits you receive from investing your time and money in this book is for you to embrace the experience. Imagine you are about to travel through *The Twilight Zone*, fall down the rabbit hole, skip head down the Yellow Brick Road to the *Land of Oz*. Don't be xenophobic.

Skim through our book once and mark the parts that you think will help you the most. Then go through your book again and make some notes to help you quickly and easily start your wealth strategy.

Introduction

I don't do it for the money. I've got enough, much more than I'll ever need. I do it to do it. Deals are my art form. Other people paint beautifully on canvas or write wonderful poetry. I like making deals, preferably big deals. That's how I get my kicks.

— Donald J. Trump
The Art of the Deal (1987)

You do not need to be an economist to get rich —in fact many economists never get rich. You need to have the "x-factor" — something that very few have. You cannot get it in this book or in any book. You cannot get it by jumping up and down on stage at a success seminar. It is a gift from God. And if you have the "x-factor" you know it.

I n the months following China's cowardly and intentional attack on the world we have been forced to adapt daily to survive. The operative word is **pivot**. Many businesses have closed, and some will never again open. Others have become zombies.

There is no reason to remind you of the nightmare because you are living it. Each of us are impacted in a unique way. Contrary to corporate clichés like "we're all in it together" — we were not all in it together. The experience has torn many of us apart.

As our book is published America's economy is struggling to reopen. Although many individuals and companies have taken big financial hits some sectors have not yet been affected — we have only seen the beginning.

Retail, restaurants, and airlines among others have taken a big hit. The stock market appears Teflon, but real estate may soon start to feel the burn.

Your ability to build and secure tremendous wealth depends on how and when you act. You have all the tools — just add your magic. Do not let anyone get you off the market.

ONE
DREAMLAND

And I don't know a soul who's not been
battered.
I don't have a friend who feels at ease.
I don't know a dream that's not been
shattered or driven to its knees.
But it's all right, it's all right
We've lived so well so long
Still, when I think of the road we're
traveling on
I wonder what went wrong
I can't help it, I wonder what went wrong

— Paul Simon
American Tune (1973)
Paul Simon

*Do not allow the pandemic or anything or
anyone to shatter your dreams. Hold on tight
to your dreams — all of them. America is
the Land of Dreams — let's keep it that way.*

America is the
Land of Dreams.

Once upon a time, not so very long ago, there existed a wonderful and magical land.

There was, perhaps, no other land on earth like this one. It was truly a paradise that seemed to have everything. Its face spread from ocean to ocean and there were sun-drenched beaches — some sandy and some rocky. There were countless peaks reaching for the stars and begging to be climbed. There were deep forests and great plains. There were endless deserts, grand canyons, and vast valleys. There were enormous lakes, fast moving streams, and slow-moving rivers filled with fresh clean water to drink and fish to eat — and to travel throughout the land.

America was home to amazing creatures — great and small — ancient horses, supersized armadillos, mastodons, mammoths, short-faced bears, dire wolves, cheetahs, ground sloths, giant beavers, and camels.

Most of these animals, and many others, were here to welcome the first humans arriving in America some 17,000 to 14,000 years ago. Natural beauty was everywhere in this virgin Land of Dreams.

No one really knows how many Native Americans were here to greet the first foreigners when they arrived to 'discover' America. Estimates range from two million to maybe twenty million. And the same goes for guessing how many "tribes" there were.

Native American economies were not much different than other economies in modern history. Native Americans shared the same fundamental challenges of survival and creatively used available natural resources, labor, and capital. Over centuries, they learned what to produce, how to produce it, and how to distribute their unique goods and services.

There were probably hundreds of different societies in pre-Columbian America. From what we understand, they had two things in common — they respected the land they shared and they respected one another. Native Americans developed a sophisticated system of trade. They exchanged food and decorative and ceremonial objects. The Native American economies grew without destroying the environment. Natural and human resources were utilized efficiently. Native American economics was simple.

DREAMLAND

Dreamland is the story of the first four hundred years of the American Experience. The American Dream was mostly shaped in our first three hundred years. By the end of the second world war we were producing one half of the world's goods and services, held two-thirds of the world's gold reserves, and three-fourths of the world's investment capital.

What made America great and, more importantly, what happened to us leading up to and during the pandemic and mass hysteria? How did we allow fear to bring us to our knees? Why did our elected leaders let mobs rampage across America destroying our culture, history, and economy?

1

COMING TO AMERICA

Got a dream to take them there
They're coming to America
Got a dream they've come to share
They're coming to America

— Neil Diamond
America (1981)
Neil Diamond

The last line of an 1886 Statue of Liberty dedication speech read:

There is room in America and brotherhood for all who will support our institutions and aid in our development. But those who come to disturb our peace and dethrown our laws are aliens and enemies forever.

CHALLENGE
When did your ancestors come to America?

_____

_____

And then we came to America. At first from Europe and then from all over the world.

Traditional historians would like you to believe that immigrants came to America seeking religious freedom. The truth is that immigration to America was, is, and always will be about **economic opportunity**.

British colonization of the Americas began in the late 1500's and was followed by the Dutch, French, Spanish, Portuguese, and even the Russians.

Coming to America from all over the world we built the most powerful and prosperous economy history of with blood, sweat, and tears driven by blind greed.

We built cities and towns and factories and stores. Fortunes were made — and lost — overnight. We created an infrastructure and that encouraged innovation, investment, and entrepreneurship. Financial markets operated with minimal government intervention. All this came at high social and environmental costs — and we may be paying the price for our mistakes forever.

2

ONE BRIEF SHINING MOMENT

Don't let it be forgot that once there was a spot, for once brief shining moment, that was known as Camelot.

— King Arthur (Richard Harris)
Camelot (1967)
Alan J. Lerner and Frederick Loewe

According to Oliver Stone's 'Untold History of the United States' (2012):

At the end of World War II, the United States economy was booming. Exports more than doubled pre-war levels. America was producing 50% of the world's goods and services. Industrial production had grown 15% annually. We held two-thirds of the world's gold reserves and three-fourths of its investment capital.

CHALLENGE
Watch *Camelot.*

From 1945 to 1960 we experienced an amazing era of economic growth that far exceeded all expectations.

Weary of wartime shortages and sacrifices, America rapidly pivoted from producing guns to making butter. We cashed in war bonds and started buying everything in sight.

By the time the sixties arrived the face of America reflected a new prosperity. We drove around in gas guzzling cars that looked like spaceships. Our waists and bank accounts started getting fatter.

The election of 1960 pitted 'New America' against "The Establishment" and we began anew with a charismatic young president leading a **New Generation of Americans.**
That brief shining moment of hope was short lived. As the American economy continued to heat up so did the Cold War. We built bomb shelters in our back yards and lived under the threat of global thermonuclear war.

The decade that started out with Camelot ended with three political assassinations and Charlie Manson trying to start a race war. **Woodstock** and the **Summer of Love** faded.

3
WHILE AMERICA SLEPT

A long long time ago
I can still remember how
That music used to make me smile
And I knew if I had my chance
That I could make those people dance
And maybe they'd be happy for a while

But February made me shiver
With every paper I'd deliver
Bad news on the doorstep
I couldn't take one more step

— Don McLean
American Pie (1971)
Don McLean

Winston Churchill's book "While England Slept" (1938) highlighted the United Kingdom's failure to recognize and prepare for the threat of Nazi Germany. That is exactly what we did with China.

15

The sixty years following the nineteen sixties was the most self-destructive period of the American experience up until now. Let's look back and learn what went wrong. The euphoria of post-war conquest quickly began to give way to fear. America's false sense of security was based on military and economic strength. Our Achille's Heel was own greed and paranoia. We allowed ourselves to be manipulated by the media and believed the lies and exaggerations of our elected leaders.

Our **Happy Days** and **Wonder Years** disappeared in the mud and smoke of **Woodstock** and were replaced with one war after another. And our **wars on terror** became endless.

The greatest and most powerful nation in the world experienced a metamorphosis that revealed our ugliest secrets. Americans consumed like every day was Black Friday. We tried to keep up with the Joneses on Facebook posting pics of luxury cars and self-promoting posts. While America slept China planned our economic collapse. They loaned or bought their way into almost everywhere on the face of the globe.

16

4
GREY SWAN LANDING

In economic life and history more generally, just about everything of consequence comes from black swans; ordinary events have paltry effects in the long term.

— Nassim Nicholas Taleb

Black Swan, White Swan, Grey Swan, Red Swan, Yellow Swan? Taleb's theory in his book "The Black Swan" introduced the whole idea of 'economic swans.' We experienced a "Grey Swan" event because it was predictable, had severe consequences and we did not take it seriously enough. We were slow to act and responded well after the nation was in a state of fearful chaos. What did we do wrong?

CHALLENGE
What color was the Swan?

The Chinese took advantage of the virus to deliberately and maliciously impose the maximum damage to the American people and to our economy.

On September 21, 1949 Communist Party Chairman Mao Zedong proclaimed the establishment of the **People's Republic of China** and the Chinese set their sights on the world's most powerful nation by whatever means necessary.

Over the ensuing seventy years America became fat, arrogant, and complacent. The Chinese have closely watched and studied us and have waited for an opportunity to attack.

In 1972 President Richard Nixon visited China to leverage our influence over the Soviet Union. In 1979 the United States established full diplomatic ties with the People's Republic of China.

The virus will not destroy the Chinese economy. China has a massive population, vast resources, amazing biodiversity and, most importantly, patience. America must wake up and realize China's increasing threat. We must to unite and fight back.

18

5

CHINESE FIRE DRILLS

I fear all we have done is to awaken a sleeping giant and fill him with a terrible resolve.

— Isoroku Yamamoto
Admiral of the Imperial Japanese Navy

Like Japan's sneak attack on Pearl Harbor, China coldly and strategically leveraged their virus in a attempt to paralyze and seriously damage the American economy.

CHALLENGE
Think about the economic impact that the pandemic has had on your life. How can you use the experience to motivate you to improve your financial situation and better prepare for your future. How much cash reserves should you have?

_____

_____

_____

_____

America's response to the pandemic was embarrassing, disappointing, and devastating. The attack was accompanied by an *infodemic* fueled by fake news and **fuzzy math**. The net result was chaotic global disorder.

The virus descended on the United States and the rest of the globe carried first-class on-**Air China** and dozens of other airlines. And while all this was happening China and the World Health Organization conspired to mislead and confuse the people of the world.

Caught entirely off-guard the world began a series of **Chinese fire drills** in a desperate effort to protect itself. But it was too little and way too late. The cat was out of the bag and people started dying in alarming numbers.

In a feeble attempt to make things worse, if that was possible, the Chinese denied all responsibility and tried blaming the United States.

The economic cost to the world is beyond calculation and although not fatal will be significant and long lasting. American taxpayers will have a big bill to pay.

6

STAYIN' ALIVE

Whether you're a brother or whether you're
a mother
You're stayin' alive, stayin' alive
Feel the city breakin' and everybody
shakin'
And we're stayin' alive, stayin' alive
Ah, ha, ha, ha, stayin' alive, stayin' alive
Ah, ha, ha, ha, stayin' alive

— Bee Gees
Stayin' Alive (1977)
Barry, Robin, and Maurice Gibb

Suddenly we were in lockdown. America and the world went into survival mode. Life was simply stayin' alive and nothing more. We learned new jargon that included 'social distancing' and donned masks and gloves.

CHALLENGE
Imagine John Travolta and "The Faces" dancing at Studio 54 with masks and social distancing.

21

We entered "... the middle ground between light and shadow, between science and superstition, and between the pit of man's fears and the summit of his knowledge. This is the dimension of imagination. We are in a mashup of *Twilight Zone* episodes. We found ourselves in a science fiction movie or video game. Social distancing and social media took the place of socializing and social isolation put us all on edge.

The economic costs of the pandemic were immediate and uncertain. But the biggest cost was emotional. We went from running at full speed to a near shutdown.

The psychological effects to many of us will be longstanding. Depression and anxiety are common and some of us will never entirely recover from this experience.

For some of us the biggest challenge will be restarting our lives and careers. It is often difficult to get back into our normal routines after being forced to slow down.

There are really no options other than to try to pivot, be flexible. and reinvent ourselves.

7
Chinese Checkers

The world is paying a very high price for what they did.

— Donald J. Trump
March 19, 2020

Chinese Checkers is a strategy board game of German origin invented in the 1920's and has nothing to do with China. The game has players going into different directions and can be confusing.

CHALLENGE
If you were to design a game about your life how would it be? Would it be a board game or a video game? Who would be the players? What would be the risks and rewards? What would you call your game?

_____

_____

_____

_____

_____

With the outbreak of the virus almost 8 billion people from around 200 countries began scrambling for survival in a game of global **Chinese Checkers** manipulated by politicians and the media.

Rules changed hourly and sometimes there were no rules at all. When there were rules some people chose to be defiant just because they could.

Once the world is completely reopened the real game of Chinese Checkers will be an economic one. Countries and companies will start scrambling for position.

The world's economic winners will be those people, companies, and countries who quickly discover how to innovate and adapt.

All of us will pay an extremely high price for what the Chinese did but we must realize that there is nothing that we can do but move forward with our lives.

The cost of anything is how much of our lives must be exchanged for it. This pandemic has been costly, but we will recover financially.

8
BURN BABY BURN

Immigrants and faggots
They make no sense to me
They come to our country
And think they'll do as they please
Like start some mini-Iran
Or spread some fucking disease

— Guns N' Roses
One in a Million (1988)
Guns N' Roses

The burning and rioting made no sense at all and came at a cost of billions of dollars to the American economy.

CHALLENGE
Pick a riot on the news and estimate its economic impact. How much was property damage? How much was lost to looters? What was the cleanup cost? What were the costs of government services? Include lost wages. Then factor in *the velocity of money* and what do you have?

We may never know the real reason that tens of thousands of people took to the streets to riot, burn and loot. There is probably not one reason. Most likely it is a combination of things disguised as protest of police abuse and racial injustice fueled by frustration.

The economics of riots are simple but rarely addressed. First is the cost of property destroyed. Second is the cost of goods stolen by looters. Third is the cost of government services (police, fire, paramedic, ambulance). Fourth are medical costs for those injured and funeral costs for those who die in riots. Fifth is the loss of wages. Sixth is the cost of cleanup.

Some costs are covered by insurance which results in increased premiums. The costs absorbed by businesses is eventually passed on to consumers. The cost of government services that is not recovered from insurers or business owners is borne by taxpayers.

Riots are socially, environmentally, and economically expensive. However, rioters are oblivious to these costs and self-centered on their own special interests.

9
HELTER SKELTER

Charlie interpreted the song to mean the Beatles were telling blackie to get guns and kill whitey.

— Vincent Bugliosi
Helter Skelter:
The True Story of the Manson Murders
(1974)

Don McLean's "American Pie" includes a line "Helter skelter in a summer swelter" which some believe is a reference to Charlie Manson who is reported as having predicted an apocalyptic war arising from racial tensions between blacks and whites.

CHALLENGE
Listen to the long version of *American Pie. Where were you the day the music died?*

_____
_____
_____
_____

Oliver Stone's *Untold History of the United States* reminds us of the fall of modern empires including England, Spain, France, Germany, Japan and the Soviet Union We should not be seriously contemplating the collapse of the United States and China.

The national defense systems of both countries are virtually impenetrable from the outside. What we first knew as Reagan's **Star Wars** defense system has evolved into something out of a science fiction movie.

A **triple canopy** of ultra-sophisticated surveillance and defense systems and fleets of **armed drones** protects the sky from the lower stratosphere to the exo-atmosphere

The real threat to America is not external. The real threat to America is our own fear, greed, and hatred. We are on the edge of **Helter Skelter** being strategically and aggressively provoked by professional agitators backed by big money — domestic terrorists. We are not going to allow anyone to divide our nation. We will come together in a spirit of unity. We must stand up to rioting, looting, and murders and quickly address our issues.

10
ANIMAL FARM

…they had come to a time when no one dared speak his mind, when fierce, growling dogs roamed everywhere, and when you had to watch your comrades torn to pieces after confessing to shocking crimes.

— George Orwell
Animal Farm (1945)

History will long wonder why we sat back and allowed people to take over, occupy, and destroy property that was not theirs.

CHALLENGE
Google "Understanding Capitalist vs. Socialist Economics". Most countries have mixed economies with elements of both capitalism and socialism.

_____
_____
_____
_____
_____

The economic cost of **autonomous zones** is high because they are not self-sufficient. First, they are illegally occupying properties that are not theirs and therefore have prohibited the planned and normal use of those properties. There is a loss of income, lost wages, and the cost of damages and theft.

Second, because they are not self-sufficient there are public services that are usually provided at the taxpayers' expense. These include health and safety services, law enforcement, fire, and emergency services.

Seattle's CHAZ or CHOP was much different than **Occupy Wall Street**. It started out with a mob mentality and resulted in death, injury, and the senseless destruction of both public and private property.

Like all the demonstrations, protests, riots, and looting that proceeded it, CHAZ may have started out with some semblance of idealism that was exploited by manipulative forces.

Nothing was accomplished in Seattle except costing taxpayers and business owners millions, if not billions, of dollars.

11
FAHRENHEIT 451

Every record has been destroyed or falsified, every book rewritten, every picture has been repainted, every statue and street building has been renamed, every date has been altered. And the process is continuing day by day and minute by minute. History has stopped. Nothing exists except an endless present in which the Party is always right.

— George Orwell
1984 (1949)

History cannot be rewritten. Books can be burned, and statues can be torn down but history can never be rewritten.

CHALLENGE
If you could rewrite history what would you cancel?

_____
_____
_____

Ignorance and insanity is the only way to describe what is happening in America and why we are allowing it to happen.

There is absolutely no rhyme or reason to the wholesale destruction of America's history right before our eyes.

Those of us who grew up in America had two portraits in our classrooms: **George Washington** and **Abraham Lincoln**. Now there are those who would have us believe that both of those presidents along with just about every person in our back pages was a racist and committed every deadly sin.

At an exorbitant cost to the economy statues, monuments, and portraits are being torn down and destroyed. Schools and streets and public places are being renamed. Syrup bottles and rice packages are being modified. Walt Disney's **Uncle Remus** will be the next victim of cancel culture along with **Amos and Andy,** and **Fred Sanford.**

Little Black Sambo was about a boy in India not Africa, Harlem or South Central. All the little boy wanted was pancakes and he was erased from history.

32

12
¿Y Ahora Qué?

Call in three months time and I'll be fine,
   I know
Well maybe not that fine
But I'll survive anyhow
I won't recall the names and places of each
   sad occasion
But that's no consolation here and now
So what happens now?

— Evita (Madonna)
Another Suitcase in Another Hall (1997)
Tim Rice

---

*Someday soon the virus will come under
control and the masks and gloves will come
off and we'll ask, "now what?".*

CHALLENGE
What happens now?

_____

_____

_____

Murphy's Law reigned over the Chinese Virus experience. In effect anything that could have gone wrong went wrong.

We were ill prepared and responded slowly and in an uncoordinated manner. We received a steady stream of misinformation from a manipulative liberal media and politicians who were afraid of their own shadows. Many of us became stir crazy and took to the streets for a multitude of reasons.

So now what? We will probably live under the threat of this virus for months, if not years, to come. Our world will never be the same. And that is good along with being bad. Maybe it is neither good nor bad — maybe is it just what it is.

Like Paul Simon sings in *You Can Call Me Al* (1986): "There were incidents and accidents. There were hints and allegations." Fine. Let's get over it and move on.

What are we going to do next? Are we going to reprint our currency without any portraits because everyone is a "bad hombre" Let's save — not cancel — the American Dream.

TWO
WEALTH

Before you can become a millionaire, you must learn to think like one. You must learn how to motivate yourself to counter fear with courage. Making critical decisions about your career, business, investments and other resources conjures up fear, fear that is part of the process of becoming a financial success.

— Thomas J. Stanley

Wealth has several components including: Money, Power, Influence, Freedom, Health, and Happiness. Wealth is relative and highly subjective.

CHALLENGE
Which wealth component is most important to you?

_____

_____

_____

BUILD
AND
SECURE
TREMENDOUS
WEALTH
AS AN INVESTOR,
ENTREPRENEUR,
OR ADVISOR.

WEALTH

Thomas Jefferson incorporated English philosopher John Locke's "pursuit of happiness" into his statement of unalienable rights of **"life, liberty, and the pursuit of happiness"** in the Declaration of Independence of the United States of America. "The pursuit of happiness" for most people means the pursuit of **wealth**.

When all the smoke clears, we will again build great wealth. Investors, Entrepreneurs and Advisors will lead an economic renaissance in America that will outshine our post WWII economy.

This time, hopefully, we will be more responsible to our society and environment.

13

GREED

The point is, ladies and gentleman, that greed, for lack of a better word, is good. Greed is right, greed works. Greed clarifies, cuts through, and captures the essence of the evolutionary spirit. Greed, in all of its forms; greed for life, for money, for love, knowledge has marked the upward surge of mankind.

— Gordon Gekko (Michael Douglas)
Wall Street (1987)

Greed and Fear drive our actions and financial decisions. An economy is a pure reflection of emotions. Greed can be addicting and Fear can be paralyzing.

CHALLENGE
What is the greatest influence on your financial decisions and actions — fear or greed?

Greed can be either good or bad. For our purposes here let's assume that greed is good. Let's assume that greed is the force behind the pursuit of happiness — also known as wealth.

Greed is sometimes more than financially motivated and can include a desire for power and fame. **Innovators** usually are not as concerned about money as they are are about creating something that has never existed before.

Investors are motivated by FOMO — the fear of missing out. Greed can destroy investors.

Entrepreneurs take the most risk but can earn the highest return on investment. Greed is not as much of a driving force with entrepreneurs as are the desire for independence and need to create.

Advisors are probable the least greedy because money naturally comes easy to the best advisors. They do not need to be greedy but often must tell clients what happens when hogs eat too much cabbage.

Were *The Beverly Hillbillies* greedy?

40

14
INVESTMENTS

It is impossible to produce superior performance unless you do something different from the majority.

— John Templeton

There are many types of Investments including: Stocks, Bonds, Mutual Funds, Exchange-Traded Funds, Options, Annuities, Commodities, Foreign Exchange, and Cryptocurrencies.

CHALLENGE

Make a list of the best investments you have ever made and forget about your bad ones.

The first rule of investing is to realize that there are two sides to every investment transaction — the buyer and the seller. If the seller is willing to sell a stock for $100 that means that he has either made a profit, is cutting his losses short, or has a better place for his money. The willing buyer believes that the stock has the potential to command a higher price and is willing to risk the price going down to realize a gain. The relationship between the risk and return is known as the **risk/reward ratio.**

ROI (return on investment) measures performance and is used to evaluate the efficiency of an investment, to compare different investments. or classes of investments. ROI is expressed as a ratio. A ratio of 2:1 means that you would double your money or receive $200 for every $100 invested. If you were to earn $25 on a $100 investment, then you would have a 25% ROI.

Successful investing demands skill, talent, time, experience, capital, discipline, and opportunity. Unless you have all of these you should seek the advice of a licensed advisor. Beware of commissioned salespeople and anyone who sells only proprietary products.

15
REAL ESTATE

Landlords grow rich in their sleep without working, risking or economizing.

— John Stuart Mill
English Philosopher and Economist

Your home is not an investment, but you can invest in Residential and Commercial Real Estate and Land.

CHALLENGE
Where are the opportunities for investing in a duplex, triplex or fourplex within fifty miles of where you live? Do you have what it takes to build and manage a portfolio of income properties?

_____
_____
_____
_____
_____
_____
_____
_____

Many of the greatest fortunes in history have been made by investing in real estate. The pandemic will bring opportunities to create tremendous wealth and income in real estate. The pandemic accelerated existing disruption to an already rapidly evolving real estate industry that was unexpectedly forced to adapt to a virtual world.

Real estate investing has traditionally been a buffer against riskier investments and real estate will continue to be a hot market. Buyers and sellers have slowed down their timing but will be back in the game as the economy reopens.

Before the crisis paralyzed America, the housing market faced a supply shortage. Although economic uncertainty and social distancing have negatively impacted home sales the hit to home prices may be delayed and is highly unpredictable.

The residential real estate market should continue to benefit from low mortgage rates. Asian buyers will continue to fade away and are being replaced by investors from Europe and Latin America.

16

INSURANCE

I don't want to tell you how much insurance I carry with the Prudential, but all I can say is: when I go, they go too.

— Jack Benny

Insurance can be used for Estate Planning, Tax Planning, Protection, Investing and Retirement Strategies, and Income.

CHALLENGE
When was the last time you had your insurance portfolio reviewed?

_____
_____
_____
_____
_____
_____
_____
_____
_____
_____

Insurance has always played a critical role in the economy providing many ways to build and protect wealth.

The pandemic's devastating economic impact should serve as a wake-up call to individuals, businesses, and governments. Insurance coverage could have mitigated some of the losses.

Indexed annuities are a type of annuity with tax deferred interest being credited based on a market index like the S&P 500. There is a minimum interest rate guaranteed to protect against loss of principal if the investment is held to the end of the surrender term. These are also known as hybrid or equity indexed annuities and can be complicated. They can provide growth opportunities to certain investors, but it is important to know what you are buying. The same goes for all insurance products whether they are life, health, accident insurance or property and casualty coverage.

The net effect of the pandemic will be an increase in sales of insurance products as well as an increase of premiums caused by additional policy claims.

17
BUSINESS OWNERSHIP

A big business starts small.

— Richard Branson

Owning a business can provide you an opportunity to create tremendous wealth and considerable income by leveraging your talents and passionately pursuing your dreams.

CHALLENGE

How many small and medium sized business owners are making money versus the ones who have just created jobs for themselves and their families?

_____

_____

_____

_____

_____

_____

_____

_____

Business ownership offers you the most potential for creating great wealth. In addition to making money owning a business has other advantages. But it is not as easy as it sounds. It can be a road to heaven or to hell depending on you.

If you are already a business owner, you may be facing great challenges or have access to tremendous opportunities — depending on how you look at it. Many great fortunes are made in the worst of times. This is when you need to evaluate every aspect of your business, make a plan which is both realistic and agile, and take immediate steps not only to survive but to prosper during and after the pandemic.

If you do not own a business, there are several options open to you. You can choose to be a passive investor in a business or active investor. The difference is how much you will be involved in the management and operations of the business.

And you can choose to invest in a successful business or a turnaround situation. But probably the riskiest is a decision to start a business from scratch.

18
HAPPINESS

Here's a little song I wrote
You might want to sing it note by note
Don't worry, be happy
In every life we have some trouble
But when you worry you make it double
Don't worry, be happy
Don't worry, be happy now

— Bobby McFerrin
Don't Worry Be Happy
Bobby McFerrin (1988)

Happiness is the greatest wealth. Without happiness Wealth means nothing.

CHALLENGE
Does singing Bobby McFerrin's song *Don't Worry Be Happy* make you happy?

_____
_____
_____
_____
_____

A Google search of **happiness** returns 785 million results in one-half second. Happiness has as many meanings as there are people alive on the earth at any given time.

British psychologist Oliver James published a book in 2007 titled *Affluenza* that described an obsessive, envious, keeping-up-with-the - Joneses epidemic that causes depression and anxiety — the opposite of **happiness**.

Social media and Madison Avenue have convinced consumer driven societies that happiness revolves around the pursuit of things — from designer sunglasses to luxury vehicles. Happiness comes from within and not from the accumulation of consumer goods. And wealth itself does not guarantee happiness.

What are the economics of happiness? Have the traditional principles of economics changed as the current pandemic has joined the "affluenza" epidemic?

The pursuit of material happiness drives prosperity because it equates to spending — and prosperity helps make people happy.

THREE

WINGED BULLS

Here's to the crazy ones. The misfits. The rebels. The troublemakers. The round pegs in the square holes. Those who see things differently. They're not fond of rules. And they have no respect for the status quo. You can quote them, disagree with them, glorify or vilify them. About the only thing you can't do is ignore them. Because they change things. They push the human race forward. And while some may see them as the crazy ones, we see genius. Because the people who are crazy enough to think they can change the world are the ones who do.

—Steve Jobs

Human-headed Winged Bulls guarded wealth and protected against enemies in ancient times.

WINGED BULLS

are

Socially Responsible

INNOVATORS,

INVESTORS,

ENTREPRENEURS

and

ADVISORS

WINGED BULLS

Bulls and bears are the traditional mascots of Wall Street. Bulls represent upward market movements and bears represent downward movements. Optimistic investors are called bullish and pessimistic investors are called bears.

Modern **winged bulls** are the socially and environmentally responsible **Innovators, Investors, Entrepreneurs,** and **Advisors.**

Innovators find ways of doing, to push boundaries, and effect positive change. **Investors, Entrepreneurs,** and **Advisors** will complement the efforts of **Innovators** to build a roaring **C19 Economy** that will overshadow our post WWII recovery.

19
SOCIAL RESPONSIBILITY

If there is shit all around me, how can I eat my ice cream.

— S. Balaram

Social Responsibility is not Socialism.

CHALLENGE

Do you think that social responsibility is for "tree huggers"? When buying things or making investments do you think about social and environmental issues? Do you believe it is possible to be a socially responsible buyer or investor — or does that just exist in fantasyland?

_____
_____
_____
_____
_____
_____
_____
_____
_____

S ocial responsibility is the concept that individuals, companies and governments have an ethical obligation to act for the benefit of society at large as to maintain an equitable balance between the economy and the environment.

Individual social responsibility is rooted in personal morals and values and is voluntary. Government social responsibility is driven by the vote of confidence granted by voters and dependent on our government's three branches — executive, legislative, and judicial in what is sometimes a random order of priorities.

Corporate social responsibility programs are designed to benefit society in four areas: **Economy, Environment, Philanthropy,** and **Ethics.** Corporate social responsibility is not as simple as it sounds and most often initiatives are profit driven rather than benefit driven.

There are conflicts between "doing the right thing" and the economic costs involved. An American chemical company complying with standards of social responsibility and EPA regulations cannot compete with China.

20
Innovators

There's a way to do it better — find it.

— Thomas Edison

Innovation is combining things that already exist in a way that something new and better is created.

CHALLENGE
Do you have an innovative idea for a product or service? Why don't you create a business plan and get some partners or investors?

_____
_____
_____
_____
_____
_____
_____
_____
_____
_____
_____

Innovation is a term that is often inflated and grossly misunderstood. In the interest of gaining a clear understanding of who innovators are and what they do, let's take a look at the various types of innovation:

Strategy

Defining the desired object of innovation and degree of innovation.

Process

A radical innovation requires a more comprehensive process than an incremental process.

Product and Services

A perpetual pursuit to introduce new products and services to the marketplace.

Busines Model

Unique modifications to marketing, supply chains, pricing, and value.

Technology

Leveraging tech to improve quality, develop new products and services and/or market digitally.

Systems

Optimizing company organizational and management structure.

Social and Environmental

Socially responsible benefits to the public and the environment.

21
INVESTORS

The investor's chief problem — and even his worst enemy — is likely to be himself.

— Benjamin Graham
British-born American Economist

Investors play a critical role in the economy by funding startups and providing capital that gives companies unlimited growth opportunities.

CHALLENGE
What is your ideal risk/reward ratio? How much are you willing to risk in exchange for what return?

_____
_____
_____
_____
_____
_____
_____
_____
_____

C **19 Economics** is based on the concept that money is the mother's milk of an economy and that **active investors** will provide capital regardless of market conditions or direction.

Most people are either principally **consumers** or **investors.** While consumer spending fuels economic growth it inhibits the creation of personal wealth. **Consumers** are usually wage earners living from paycheck to paycheck, hoping to inherit money or waiting to win the lottery. They have no savings or investment plans. They make consumption a priority over building and protecting personal wealth.

Investors can be passive or active. **Passive investors** do not need much skill. They submissively ride the investment roller coaster up and down hoping they will eventually make money.

Active investors take advantage of market inefficiencies to profit because they believe that building wealth is all about maximum return on capital. Active investing demands time, talent, discipline, and experience. If you do not have all four then you should seek help from a licensed professional who does.

22
ENTREPRENEURS

A real entrepreneur is somebody who has no safety net under them.

— Henry Kravis

Entrepreneurs generate investment capital, create jobs, provide diversified products and services, and contribute to the prosperity of America.

CHALLENGE
Do you believe in "The American Dream"? Are entrepreneurs successful because they work hard or for other reasons — like working smart?

_____
_____
_____
_____
_____
_____
_____
_____
_____

Entrepreneurs will combine the vision of **innovators** with the capital of **investors** and their own passion to make the American economy great again in spite of China's brazen attack and the efforts of internal agitators to create mass hysteria and paralyze our economy and society. There are two distinct types of entrepreneurs:

Small Businesses

Most small busines entrepreneurs are merely creating a job for themselves and are most likely to create a profit that supports their family and a modest lifestyle. Small business entrepreneurs usually own and run their own business and hire local employees and family members. Small businesses are the heart of the American economy.

Larger Company Entrepreneurship

Many successful small businesses are eventually acquired by large companies or begin as scalable startups that seek rapid expansion and are capable of attracting investors to provide the capital they need. In addition to capital they require the expertise of experienced leadership which often comes from C-level executives. The dream of most small business founders is to go large.

23

ADVISORS

Wall Street is the only place that people ride to in a Rolls Royce to get advice from those who take the subway.

— Warren Buffett

The new generation of Advisors are virtual partners who manage client expectations and ease their concerns.

CHALLENGE
Make a list of advisors that you know and then circle the advisors that you trust. How many are there?

_____
_____
_____
_____
_____
_____
_____
_____
_____

Advisors are the wizards or magicians who will ultimately inform, inspire and help the **Innovators, Investors,** and **Entrepreneurs** will mold the **C19 Economy** into one unlike any before. Now more than ever Americans need advice they can trust from professionals who are experienced, passionate, and ethical.

There are three opportunities for trusted advisors in the **New Economy.** First, there is approximately $70,000,000,000 (with a T) of wealth transferring from baby boomers to their heirs in the next twenty years. The benefactors of this **great wealth transfer** will want advisors from their own peer groups.

Second there are going to be increasing opportunities for advisors who speak both English and Spanish and understand the Latino community. As Asian investors keep away from United States real estate there will be an enormous wave of investors coming from **Latin America** to invest in income properties in Latino communities in the United States.

Third is the unpresented demand for advisors in the **small and medium business** space.

64

24
THE NEW ECONOMY

You never change things by fighting the existing reality. To change something, build a new model that makes the existing model obsolete.

— Buckminster Fuller

The New Economy will continue to evolve in anticipation of emerging trends in consumer behavior and consumption.

CHALLENGE
What will be the emerging trends in the new economy and how do you plan to capitalize on them?

_____
_____
_____
_____
_____
_____
_____
_____

The New Economy will be comprised of **Madmen Financiers** and **Zombie Companies** — and driven by the vision of **Innovators**, the greed of **Investors**, the passion of **Entrepreneurs**, and the wisdom of **Advisors**.

We are experiencing an unexpected paradigm shift away from globalization — characterized by the diminished dominance of China — toward regionalization and increased self-reliance brought about by a Grey Swan. The world was deliberately attacked by China and the world screeched to a halt. The result was a rapid and radical restructuring of many of the world's markets and dramatic changes in how we utilize human, capital and natural resources, produce, distribute and consume goods and services and create, protect and transfer wealth.

The New Economy is one of hope and change and America is experiencing some of the same challenges we faced during the Reconstruction Era after our Civil War — issues of race and equality. It is critical that we rapidly reconcile our differences and work together to get our economy moving again.

66

FOUR
ROAD TO MILLIONS

My uncle was the first brown person to have a market stall on Petticoat Lane in the 1960s. He worked his way up from the street. He was homeless, but eventually he got a car so he could sell from the boot. And by the 1980s, he was a millionaire wholesaling to companies like Topshop. So in a way, fashion put me in England.

— M.I.A.

No two roads to millions are identical. While they may all have the same destination, the journeys are as different as day and night.

CHALLENGE
Have you begun your journey on the road to millions? When do you expect to arrive and how are you planning to get there?

_____
_____
_____

ONE THOUSAND DOLLARS DOUBLED TEN TIMES BECOMES ONE MILLION DOLLARS.

ROAD TO MILLIONS

Your road to millions begins with having a burning desire to become not just rich but super rich. You and your family deserve a life of health, wealth, and happiness. But you must forget about the myth of the American Dream. You do not get rich by working hard — you get rich by working smart. And you might even completely forget about the whole concept of working — simply focus on living the now and pursuing your dreams.

Stay positive and open-minded while at the same time remaining hypervigilant and protecting yourself from everything and everyone with the potential for deceiving you, hijacking your energy, or stealing your money.

25
DESIRE

Human behavior flows from three main sources: desire, emotion and knowledge.

— Plato

You must have a burning desire to be wealthy — and more important — stay rich.

CHALLENGE
Make a list of your life priorities. What number is in front of "money"?

_____
_____
_____
_____
_____
_____
_____
_____
_____
_____
_____
_____

Desire is the most crucial factor in becoming wealthy. You must ignite your desire with **emotion** and fuel it with **knowledge**. Unless you have a burning desire to become wealthy and keep it burning you will never become super rich unless you win the lottery or inherit money.

No one can give you desire. Either you have it or you do not. Think about **Seabiscuit**. A small horse, Seabiscuit had a rough start in his racing career winning only ten of his first forty races. Seabiscuit became a symbol of hope to Americans during the Great Depression. Seabiscuit was injured in a race and many predicted that he would never race again. But Seabiscuit had desire — some people said he had *heart* and he made a stunning comeback and became a racing legend. The little horse was a champion.

How much do you want to be wealthy? How can you leverage your emotions and knowledge to build and create wealth as an innovator, investor, entrepreneur, or advisor?

Luck has nothing to do with it and it's not all about who you know or even what you know — it is about *heart*.

26
ART OF DECEPTION

Caveat emptor, pal.

— Mike McDermott (Matt Damon)
Rounders (1998)

A crisis is a perfect environment for fraud.

CHALLENGE
How good of a liar are you? Is there a significant
difference between lying and deception?

_____
_____
_____
_____
_____
_____
_____
_____
_____
_____
_____
_____
_____

Deceptive marketing and misleading advertising are techniques that enlist false or inaccurate information to capture the attention of consumers and persuade buyers into a business transaction that may not be beneficial to them.

Caveat emptor is a Latin term meaning "buyer beware" based on the principle that the buyer alone is responsible for verifying the quality and suitability of purchases before they are made.

Caveat venditor is the contrasting Latin term meaning "seller beware" based on the principle that the seller is responsible for any problem that the buyer might have with a product or service.

Now, perhaps more than any time in history, we live in an environment of deceit and misinformation enabled and supported by **Governments, Big Media,** and **Social Media** around the world.

The pandemic and ensuing hysteria has made us hypervigilance and we must remain cautious about all financial decisions.

27
YOUR PLAN

Our goals can only be reached through a vehicle of a plan, in which we must fervently believe, and upon which we must vigorously act. There is no other route to success.

— Pablo Picasso

Create a simple one-page Financial Plan. Review it daily and modify it as needed.

CHALLENGE
Make a bucket list with some deadlines.

_____
_____
_____
_____
_____
_____
_____
_____
_____

This book is **your guide to personal and business finance** and will help you navigate through the complexity of uncertain and challenging times with which we will most probably be faced for years if not decades to come.

The best way to take advantage of this guide is to follow these simple steps:

1 – Read this complete book.

This eclectic book was strategically designed with the sole purpose of inspiring and enabling you to immediately begin your journey to tremendous wealth.

2 – Reread this book.

Grab a notepad and go through your guide again making notes and also highlighting pages.

3 – Prepare.

At the back of your guide are some simple tools to easily and quickly help you get ready to build and protect tremendous wealth: **Invest time in your toolbox.** Set a date to begin your quest.

4 – Act.

Act on schedule and keep a **visual diary** of your journey. Begin immediately — every day that you procrastinate will cost you money. We are in the perfect storm to get rich.

28
STRATEGIES

You outwork, outthink, outscheme and outmanuever. You make no friends. You trust nobody. And you make damn sure you're the smartest guy in the room whenever the subject of money comes up.

— Uncle Pat (Ron Dean)
Cocktail (1988)

You will find some of these strategies and others in "Rainmaking: Impacting the World Through the Power of Emotions" and in "The Magic of Selling". Create a Playbook with your own strategies.

CHALLENGE
Define *BADASS*.

_____
_____
_____
_____
_____

52

Real World
BADASS
Strategies
for
WINNING

1
FUGGEDABOUTIT!

"Forget about it" is, like, if you agree with someone, you know, like "Raquel Welch is one great piece of ass. Forget about it!" But then, if you disagree, like "A Lincoln is better than a Cadillac? Forget about it!" You know? But then, it's also like if something's the greatest thing in the world, like, "Minghia! Those peppers! Forget about it!" But it's also like saying "Go to hell!" too. Like, you know, like "Hey Paulie, you got a one-inch pecker? And Paulie says "Forget about it!" Sometimes it just means "Forget about it."

— Donnie Brasco (Johnny Depp)
Donnie Brasco (1997)

Forget about everything you <u>think</u> you know about economics. The C19 Economy is based on emotion rather than principles. Open your mind to all the wonderful possibilities to create a new economy.

2
HAVE A STRATEGY

Hope is not a strategy.

— Vince Lombardi

So how can you create a strategy when there are no more valid economic principles? Start out with your "why". Why do you want to do <u>anything</u>? Do you want to make millions of dollars? Do you want to save the manatees? Do you want to create financial security for yourself and your family?

Watch Simon Sinek's YouTube Video "Start with Why." Then think about this line from Lewis Carroll's "Alice in Wonderland":

"For, you see, so many out-of-the-way things had happened lately, that Alice had begun to think that very few things indeed were really impossible."

_____
_____
_____

80

3
OUTFOX THEM

We sure outfoxed them.

— Felix the Cat

Felix the Cat, created as a cartoon character in the silent film era, has innate human traits, emotions, and intentions and is a master of psychology and gamesmanship.

The surrealistic situations that Felix faced are much like what we are going through now. The iconic cat with his black body, white face, enormous eyes, and big grin gets out of one mess after another.

Felix always carried his "Magic Bag of Tricks" that he used to outfox his opponents.

CHALLENGE
Watch a *Felix the Cat* cartoon on YouTube.

_____
_____
_____
_____

4
KNOW YOUR VALUE

A bad salesman will automatically drop his price. Bad salesmen make me sick.

— Sam Stone (Danny DeVito)
Ruthless People (1966)

What is your time worth? How much would you have to make an hour for it not to be worthwhile for you to stop and bend down to pick up a $100 bill on the sidewalk?

Let us say you want to make $1,000,000 a year working 20 hours a week for fifty weeks. That is a thousand hours which means that you need to make a $1,000 per hour (1000 x $1,000 = $1,000,000.

Keep reminding yourself what you are worth. If you do not value your time nobody will.

CHALLENGE
How much are you worth?
_____
_____
_____

5
DEFINE WHO YOU ARE

By God, I shall be a king. This is the time of King Arthur. When we shall — reach for the stars! This is the time of King Arthur when violence is not strength and compassion is not weakness.

— King Arthur (Richard Harris)
Camelot (1967)

Forget the "elevator pitch" and sixty-second commercial that you proudly recite at networking meetings. You know. It is the one that starts out with: "I help people...". You watched "Start with Why." and should be able to craft something like this: Be creative and create something you own.

"I believe there is an optimal financial solution for every deal, and I challenge the status quo by thinking creatively, reaching for the stars and coloring outside the lines to quickly close deals while providing world class experiences."

6
DECIDE WHAT YOU ARE SELLING

The only thing you've got in this world is what you can sell.

— Arthur Miller
Death of a Salesman (1949)

What are you selling (or trying to sell)? Is it a product or service, or both?

One of the biggest reasons for business failure is not selling the right products and services at the right time and at the right price.

Think about the menu at your favorite restaurant. What entices you to order the individual items listed on that menu? Are there too little offerings; or way too many (like a deli menu)? How important are the descriptions? How does price influence your ordering? You should be a "virtual menu" of products and services that constantly changes.

7
KNOW WHAT YOU'RE DEALING WITH

You may think you know what you're dealing with, but, believe me, you don't.

— Noah Cross (John Huston)
Chinatown (1974)

Like war, business is all about creating and executing winning strategies. But before you can create a strategy you must perform your due diligence and know what you are up against. If nothing else, the pandemic has taught us that anything can happen. It has completely redefined "Murphy's Law" (anything that can go wrong will go wrong).

Always know exactly what you are dealing with and all the possible scenarios that may possible play out. Have worst-case scenarios and best-case scenarios, and all the scenarios in between. Keep it as simple as possible. And remember that situations are continually changing.

8
KNOW WHO YOU'RE DEALING WITH

If you're playing a poker game and you look around the table and and can't tell who the sucker is, it's you.

— Paul Newman

How do you know who you are dealing with? These days its pretty easy to find out about people and companies. Most people start with Google and then search social media.

You can always deep dive by using one of those online services that provides a report of public information. Most professional licenses can be searched online for free and will disclose license status, expiration date, and any restrictions and disciplinary actions.

If you have an opportunity to get "up close and personal" with people, you can appraise body language and other "tells" to get a feeling of who you are dealing with.

9
CREATE YOUR EMOTIONAL BRAND

Your brand is what people say about you when you're not in the room.

— Jeff Bezos

The operative word here is "emotional". "Branding" has been a buzz word for a long time. But without emotion a brand means nothing.

Let's think about some brands. One of the most iconic emotional brands in the world is Disney. Many of us have an emotional attachment to Mickey Mouse ears and it's estimated that there have been over 100 million of them sold. And that is not counting the images of them on other merchandise. Mickey Mouse and the Magic Castle are Disney two of the most powerful emotional brands ever created.

So when you create your personal or business brand, make sure its emotional.

10
BE THE EXPERT

Be so good that they can't ignore you.

— Steve Martin

Strategy #6 is "Decide What You Are Selling" and whatever that is you need to be THE expert at that product or service.

Experts always have an opinion and express it with clarity and conviction. After stating your opinion say: "and most of the other EXPERTS agree with ME". BAM!

Obviously, we all cannot be experts at everything. You know the saying "Jack of all trades — Master of none". Choose ONE thing that you want to do better than anyone else and do everything you can to be THE EXPERT. Expertise is comprised of knowledge, talent, and experience. Invest in yourself and obtain knowledge and develop your talent.

11
BE THE PRODUCT

You are the product. You feeling something. That's what sells. Not them. Not sex. They can't do what we do, and they hate us for it.

— Don Draper (Jon Hamm)
Mad Men (Season 2)

People buy YOU. People choose to do business with you because the like and trust you. Pure and simple.

But here is the one caveat. Draw the line between "like and trust" and "friendship". If you need a friend get a Cocker Spaniel. One of the biggest mistakes many salespeople make is trying to be "friends" with their prospects and clients.

Emotionally distance yourself from your clients. Be the product but do not try to be their friend and definitely not their dog.

12
GET ON THE COVER

We'll, we're big rock singers We got golden
fingers
And were loved everywhere we go… (That
sounds like us)
We sing about beauty and we sing about
truth
At ten thousand dollars a show . . . (Right)
We take all kinds of pills that give us all
kinds of thrills
But the thrill we've never known Is the thrill
that'll getcha when you get your picture
On the cover of the Rollin' Stone

— Dr. Hook
The Cover of the Rolling Stone (1972)
Shel Silverstein

These days you do not need to get on the cover of "Rolling Stone" but you need to have a social media presence. Position your emotional brand on Facebook, Instagram, Twitter, LinkedIn and on your own website.

13
IMAGINE

I hope that we never lose sight of one thing — that it all started with a mouse.

— Walt Disney

Imagine your role in the New Economy and how you are going to impact the world as an Innovator, Investor, Entrepreneur, or Advisor.

Imagination is vital to the success of capitalism. Whatever we can imagine we can find a way to create. America was virtually built through imagination. People from all over the world arrived here imagining a life of freedom and prosperity.

Our New Economy will be created through our own imaginations. Imagine!

CHALLENGE
Listen to John Lennon's *Imagine.*

91

14
KEEP THE CUSTOMER SATISFIED

And it's the same old story
Everywhere I go I get slandered, libeled
I hear words I never heard in the Bible
And I'm so tired I'm oh, so tired
But I'm trying to keep my customers
    satisfied
Satisfied

— Paul Simon
Keep the Customer Satisfied (1969)
Paul Simon

This is a simple strategy that everyone talks about and many brag about but its easier said than done.

The customer is not always right but that is not the most important thing. What matters is the customer experience. It is not about notepads and calendars, fresh-baked chocolate chip cookies, or stupid chachkies.

CHALLENGE
How many chips do you want in your cookies?

15
BE EXTRAORDINARY

The thing about Hitchcock which is quite extraordinary for a director of that time, he had a very strong sense of his own image and publicizing himself. Just a very strong sense of himself as the character of Hitchcock.

— Toby Jones

Being "extraordinary" does not mean being a contrarian, weird, or eccentric. It does not mean wearing pink ties (although there's nothing wrong with that) or loud plaid suits (no comment).

How then can you be extraordinary? Like the chicken and the egg the question might be whether you are born extraordinary or become extraordinary. It really doesn't matter. Those who are extraordinary in the C19 Economy will create tremendous wealth.

16
SUPERSIZE YOUR DREAMS

I started out mopping the floor just like you guys. But now… now I'm washing lettuce. Soon I'll be on fries; then the grill. And pretty soon, I'll make assistant manager, and that's when the big bucks start rolling in.

— Maurice (Louie Anderson)
Coming to America (1988)

Always supersize or "Go Big". Always. All dreams are relative. We all have them and they come and go during our lifetimes. Hold on tight to your dreams — all of them.

In 2007 Donald Trump published "Think Big and Kick Ass: In Business and in Life". Obviously thinking big worked for Donald Trump and it can work for you.

What does "supersize your dreams" mean to you? Start with your basic dream and then blow it up into the biggest dream you can.

17
SELL THEM THEIR DREAMS

'Sell them their dreams,' a woman radio announcer urged a convention of display men in 1923. 'Sell them what they longed for and hoped for and almost despaired of having. Sell them hats by splashing sunlight across them. Sell them dreams — dreams of country clubs and proms and visions of what might happen if only. After all, people don't buy things to have things. They buy things to work for them. They buy hope — hope of what your merchandise will do for them. Sell them this hope and you won't have to worry about selling them goods.

— William R. Leach
Land of Desire

This one is a simple strategy. Do not try to sell people what YOU want to sell. Do not try to sell your dreams. Sell THEIR dreams. Ask "what are your dreams?" and listen.

18
WRITE A BOOK

It's a thousand pages, give or take a few. I'll be writing more in a week or two. I could make it longer if you like the style. I can change it 'round. And I want to be a paperback writer. Paperback writer.

— The Beatles
Paperback Writer (1966)
John Lennon and Paul McCartney

Why write a book? A book says a lot about its author. It says that the author took initiative, made a commitment, and saw it through. Contrary to what you may think writing a book is not as easy as it may sound. But it is doable be if you do it right.

A self-published paperback book can be an inexpensive and highly effective way to promote yourself. And you can also publish it digitally as an Kindle Book or other eBook.

19
TRUST WHO YOU ARE

After a while, you learn to ignore the names people call you and just trust who you are.

— Shrek (Mike Myers)
Shrek (2001)

The more you do or try to do the more people will trash talk about you. Fuggedaboutit! It doesn't matter. If you did not learn anything else during this shutdown you should have learned "not to sweat the small stuff" and that it is all small stuff.

Trust who you are. Believe unconditionally in yourself. That does not mean that you should be an arrogant narcissistic psychopath, but you must believe in yourself and your vision. Wherever you find spiritual strength, rely on that to constantly remind yourself who you are and why you get up each day. Make every moment of your life count.

20
STAY FOCUSED

Stay focused, go after your dreams and keep moving toward your goals.

— LL Cool

Veteran race car drivers quickly learn that they must always keep the "pedal to the metal" no matter what happens on the track. When rookie drivers see an accident on the course they automatically lift their feet off the accelerator pedal out of a sense of self-preservation. It is a natural reflex.

When champion drivers see a crash on the course they push their feet down harder because they know that most of the other drivers will probably be lifting theirs.

Like Seabiscuit, act as if you always are wearing blinders. Do not let anything get between you and the finish line. Winning is an attitude not an event.

21
CREATE YOUR OWN WORLD

If I had a world of my own, everything would be nonsense. Nothing would be what it is, because everything would be what it isn't. And, contrary wise, what is, it wouldn't be. And, what is wouldn't be, it would. You see?

— Alice
Alice's Adventure in Wonderland (1865)
Lewis Carroll

When you think about it we all create our own individual worlds every day. Create a wonderful world of opportunity, challenge, and achievement. Create your own world of wealth, health, and happiness.

Hopefully after you study these 50 Strategies you will know who you are, what you are doing, and WHY. The world you create can be beautiful or ugly. It can be fantasy or reality. Choose!

22
SURPRISE THEM

You don't understand. I want to be surprised…astonish me, sport, new info, don't care where or how you get it, just get it…

— Gordon Gekko (Michael Douglas)
Wall Street (1987)

"The element of surprise" is a key strategy of war. There are good surprises and bad surprises. Some people like surprises and others hate them. Either way surprises get attention.

Surprise people with GOOD surprises. Under promise and overdeliver. Create value by making people believe they are getting more than they are bargaining for. Astonish people. Dazzle them. Walk them across Pont Neuf, down the Champs Champs-Élysées, or up the Montmartre.

CHALLENGE
Do you like surprises?

100

23
SEDUCE THEM

I appreciate this whole seduction thing you've got going on here but let me give you a tip: I'm a sure thing.

— Vivian Ward (Julia Roberts)
Pretty Woman (1990)

Business is all about seduction. It starts at the first moment that you engage a client and should continue throughout the relationship. The moment that you stop seducing them you will start losing them.

Seduction is an art and it is something that you can't learn. Like charisma you either have it or you do not. But don't be discouraged. We all have some God-given "game" and it's just a matter of how, when and why we choose to develop and use it.

Figure out how to connect emotionally and let the process begin. Seduce them!

24
ACT AS IF

There's an important phrase that we have here, and think it's time that you all learned it. Act as if. You understand what that means? Act as if you are the fucking President of this firm. Act as if you got a 9" cock. Okay? Act as if.

— Jim Young (Ben Affleck)
Boiler Room (2000)

Have you ever taken an acting class? Method acting is a technique in which an actor aspires to achieve complete emotional identification with a role.

So, you are going to "act as if" what?

CHALLENGE
What are you going to "act as if"?

_____
_____
_____
_____
_____
_____

25
MAKE A GRAND ENTRANCE

Neither of the two people in the room paid any attention to the way I came in, although only one of them was dead.

— Raymond Chandler
The Big Sleep (1946)

Whether physically or virtually always make a grand entrance. And that applies to arriving at an event or entering a Zoom or Facebook Messenger Room.

What does that even mean? It means walking in with "attitude" or making a powerful opening remark. Making a "grand entrance" is not something that comes easily or even naturally. It requires lots of practice to polish the skill set.

CHALLENGE
How do you enter a room?

_____
_____
_____

26
KEEP IT REAL

Listen, Sherlock. While you were tucked away up here working on your ethics, I was out there busting my hump in the REAL world. And the reason guys like you got a place to teach is 'cause guys like me donate buildings.

— Thorton Melon (Rodney Dangerfield)
Back to School (1986)

Unfortunately, we live in a world of bullshit. And there has never been more of it tossed around than during this shutdown. Bullshit from every local, state, and federal governmental agency. Bullshit from the mainstream media. Bullshit all over social media. Bullshit everywhere.

These days everyone is a self-proclaimed medical or financial expert. There are coaches and gurus everywhere. And now they have all gone virtual. Keep it real!

27
DON'T LET THEM FOOL YOU

Never be distracted by people's glamorous portraits of themselves and their lives; search and dig for what really imprisons them.

— Robert Greene
The 48 Laws of Power (1998)

These "50 Strategies" were somewhat inspired by Robert Greene's 1998 book "The 48 Laws of Power" so we have included a quote from him. Pay close attention to what he is saying: "never be distracted by people's glamorous portraits of themselves and their lives."

It is the "Facebook Syndrome" — everyone posts pictures at expensive restaurants or in front of expensive cars that may or may not be theirs. "Here in my garage." by Tai Lopez is an example of marketing genius.

CHALLENGE
Are you easily fooled?

28
CREATE YOUR VISUAL STYLE

Create your own visual style… let it be unique for yourself and yet identifiable for others.

— Oscar Wilde

We live in a visual world. Visual always trumps Verbal. People judge us more by how we look than by what we say. So how do you create your own visual style. Visual style is composed of several factors including how you dress and how you move. Everything you wear, carry, or drive sends messages in addition to your facial expressions and other visual "tells."

Like an actor in makeup and wardrobe you should carefully craft your visual style to portray the right messages at the right time. Your visual style should be agile and not static. Be creative and flexible.

CHALLENGE
What is your visual style?

29
PICK YOUR PARTNERS

My father taught me many things here – he taught me in this room. He taught me: keep your friends close, but your enemies closer.

— Michael Corleone (Al Pacino)
The Godfather: Part II (1974)

Strategic or business partners are one of the most significant aspects of business. Although you cannot do everything by yourself there are situations where you might be better going solo. Partners can either be assets or liabilities.

Concerning business partners, you need to be able to trust them and be convinced that the partnership will be fair to all parties involved. If you form strategic alliances or have "referral partners' proceed with caution.

30
LOOK FOR THE NEXT COW

I don't like looking back. I'm always constantly looking forward. I'm not the one to sit and cry over spilt milk. I'm too busy looking for the next cow.

— Gordon Ramsey

Always be looking to the next deal. Don't permanently attach yourself to anything or anybody. Marriages are for romantic relationships and not for business ones.

Be quick to forget about the past and quicker to move on. Especially now there are so many deals and clients that you have choices — lots of them. And there are going to be increasingly more as the New Economy unfolds.

Create a DEAL SHEET and stay on the outlook for any deals that may match your parameters. Remain open minded.

31
SELF-CORRECT

If one dream dies, dream another dream. If you get knocked down, get back up and go again.

— Joel Osteen

Piloting a small airplane requires constant corrections to speed, direction, and altitude. Commercial aircraft are equipped with autopilot devices that are used to guide the planes without direct assistance from pilots. Autopilots maintain airspeed, keep the aircraft straight and level at the proper altitude, and keep it on the correct heading.

We all have an internal autopilot that is a combination of intuition and conscience. Allow your internal autopilot to guide your actions and keep you on course.

CHALLENGE
How do you self-correct?

_____

_____

32
ASK

Most people never pick up the phone, most people never ask. And that's what separates, sometimes, the people that do things from the people that just dream about them. You gotta act. And you gotta be willing to fail. If you're afraid of failing, you won't get very far.

— Steve Jobs

Ask for the order! Some people are like cowboys who ride around all day and round up cattle and herd them into the corral. The problem is that they do not know how to shut the gate and keep it shut once they get the cattle inside.

You can have strategies, leads, CRMs, sales funnels, coaches, and mentors. But if you don't take action and pick up the phone and ask for the order you will consistently fail. Ask for the order and you will get it.

33
MANAGE YOUR REPUTATION

Your brand name is only as good as your reputation.

— Richard Branson

At the end of each day and at the end of our lives what do we really have? All we have is our reputation. Our reputation is our legacy — and that legacy can be good or bad.

Managing your reputation and "protecting your name" can be challenging especially when you are a risk-taker. The more aggressive and the more active you are the more open you are to criticism, trash-talking, and personal and business attacks on your reputation.

Without becoming paranoid or paralyzed monitor your reputation and manage it to the best of your ability. Google yourself and be on the lookout for false information.

34
TAKE RISKS

The biggest risk is not taking any risk… In a world that's changing really quickly, the only strategy that is guaranteed to fail is not taking risks.

— Mark Zuckerberg

So, after that warning about managing your reputation do not let anything keep you from taking risks. Make one of your mottos "nothing ventured, nothing gained."

There are frivolous risks and there are calculated risks. Frivolous risks are based on emotions and calculated risks are based on reason. Most risks involve a combination of both— in varying proportions.

As we grow older we tend to program ourselves to be risk adverse. But, as toddlers learning to walk, we have a natural tendency to stand up every time we stumble and fall.

35
BE WHERE THE PUCK IS GOING

I skate to where the puck is going to be, not where it has been.

— Wayne Gretzky

"The Great One" always skates to where the puck is going. Be like the great one. You don't want to be where the puck is and especially not where the puck was. Be where the puck is going.

Unless you believe in psychic readers, mediums, and crystal balls the coming weeks, months and years will probably be the most challenging of our lifetimes.

Forget about traditional fundamental and technical analysis. Dramatically change the way you think. And stop acting entirely logically and start increasingly acting based on the emotions of The New Economy: Pure fear and greed.

36
DON'T BEG FOR BUSINESS

Save the cheap salesman talk, will ya, it's obvious.

— Gordon Gekko (Michael Douglas)
Wall Street (1987)

Do not beg for anyone's business. Do not ask people what you need to do to "earn their business". They should be "earning" your help. Seriously. Nine times out of ten "earning" someone's business means one and only one thing: dropping the price.

So how do you avoid begging for peoples' business in this increasingly competitive cutthroat business and economic environment?

Create a demand for yourself. Make people want your products and services.

CHALLENGE
Have you ever asked, "what do I have to do to earn your business?"

37
STOP PLEASING OTHERS

Alice, you cannot live your life to please others. The choice must be yours because when you step out to face that creature, you will step out alone.

— White Queen (Anne Hathaway)
Alice in Wonderland (2010)

This one compliments #36 "Don't Beg for Business". Stop pleasing others. Do not be a doormat and the object of other peoples' displaced anger.

Many of us have learned that the clients we give the most seem like the ones from whom we realize the lowest return on investment. Conversely, we usually make the most money on the clients that are the less needy and are without unnecessary drama and complications.

CHALLENGE
Are you a doormat?

115

38
STOP FOLLOWING RULES

You don't learn to walk by following rules. You learn to walk by doing, and by falling over.

— Richard Branson

Like badges, we don't need no stinkin' rules. Stop following rules. Challenge rules. The only rules are that there are no rules.

Obviously, there are some rules that you should follow like stopping at a red light and paying your taxes. But most other rules are roadblocks to your success.

You have the freedom to determine exactly which rules you choose to follow — and exactly which rules you choose to challenge or ignore. Push against rules and push as hard as you can to constantly redefine them.

CHALLENGE
Do you always follow rules — or do you follow rules selectively?

116

39
BE A CINDERELLA STORY

Cinderella story. Outta nowhere. A former greenskeeper, now, about to become the Masters champion. It looks a miracle… It's in the hole! It's in the hole! It's in the hole!

— Carl Spackler (Bill Murray)
Caddyshack (1980)

Almost everyone loves a "Cinderella Story." We love "Beauty and the Beast" and "Harry Potter" and "The Wizard of Oz" and "Alice in Wonderland" and "Peter Pan". What is our favorite land in Disneyland? Most of us love Fantasyland.

Make your life a fairy tale. Make it a Cinderella Story. Create your Pumpkin Coach and ride it to the most exciting and prosperous place it can take you. It is easy. All you must do is dream and believe. Reach for the stars — all of them — and always wash your hands for lunch.

40
CREATE HYPE – BUT DON'T BELIEVE IT

My own saying is: 'Create the hype, but don't ever believe it.'

— Simon Cowell

Never ever drink the Kool-Aid. You can mix it up and serve it. You can believe that it works. But never ever drink it.

There are salespeople who believe the hype they are fed. One of the biggest examples of this occurs in the big world of multilevel or network marketing.

All those life insurance marketing organizations with three-letter acronyms that claim to be "helping people" or "educating people" are like religious cults. They have people drinking every flavor of Kool-Aid and salivating for certificates and rings and trips. Avoid drinking the Kool-Aid and avoid serving it to others.

41
BELIEVE

The moment you doubt whether you can fly, you cease for ever to be able to do it.

— J.M. Barrie
Peter Pan (1904)

This is the most amazing strategy. It is amazingly simple but extremely difficult to achieve. We all know the story of the four-minute mile. We know the story of the Wright Brothers and their quest for manned flight. But many of us choose to be doubters and haters instead of simply just believing.

Jules Verne believed in going to the moon and journeying under the sea. He believed in travelling around the world in eighty days. Walt Disney believed in his little mouse. Steve Jobs believed in his "computer." Elon Musk believes. So does every successful entrepreneur — the unsuccessful ones stopped believing somewhere along the road.

42
MAKE AN OFFER

Michael Corleone: My father made him an offer he couldn't refuse.
Kay Adams: What was that?
Michael Corleone: Luca Brasi held a gun to his head, and my father assured him that either his brains or his signature would be on the contract.
Kay Adams: …
Michael Corleone: …That's a true story.

— *The Godfather* (1972)

Always make an offer. It may not be the right offer, but you always must make an offer. And do not play games. Make your offer one time and hold fast to that offer.

What is an offer they cannot refuse? Make your best offer based on a fair deal for all parties involved. Do not waste your time with ridiculous back and forth negotiations that go nowhere.

43
PRESS HARD – THERE ARE 3 COPIES

Only one thing counts in this world: Get them to sign on the line that is dotted.

— Blake (Alec Baldwin)
Glengarry Glen Ross (1992)

There is one and only one objective to every deal — getting it done as quickly as possible. Keep things simple. Find out what they want and determine whether you can deliver.

If you cannot get them to sign the deal then nothing else matters. Before the digital age when people were signing contracts, salespeople would tell their clients "press hard — there are 3 copies."

What is the quickest and easiest way to get them to "sign on the line that is dotted"? Do not waste time. Present an offer and ask for the business once. Either the answer will be "yes" or "no." Move on!

44
QUESTION AUTHORITY

Fellas… I don't recognize the right of this committee to ask me these kinds of questions. And, furthermore, you can all go fuck yourselves.

— Howard Prince (Woody Allen)
The Front (1976)

Question authority — question everything. We should have learned our lesson from the way that this crisis was mishandled. We were caught off guard and found ourselves in a vulnerable and highly confusing situation.

Finally, people started questioning authority because "authority" lost any credibility that it had. We probably should have questioned authority at the beginning of this crisis — but we did not. Do not become an obnoxious rebel just for the sake of rebellion but question authority.

45
BE THE LAST COCA-COLA

Anna Maria: He thinks he's the last Coca-Cola in the desert.
Lanna Lake: Honey, he is.

— Anna Maria (Cordella González)
Lanna Lake (Cathy Moriarty)
Mambo Kings (1992)

You are sometimes better to be the last in and first out. That means lay back and let the other fools rush in and chase the business before you jump in. And when you jump in be "the last Coca-Cola in the desert."

What does that mean — "the last Coca-Cola in the desert"? It means that you must present yourself as being entirely irresistible. Who would not want the last Coca-Cola in the desert? How do you make yourself irresistible? Reputation creates demand!

CHALLENGE
Watch *Mambo Kings.*

46
BE EXCLUSIVE

You want to know how to get people to trust you with their money? I'll tell you right now. You present it as an exclusive thing… Nothing on Earth makes people want something more than telling them they can't have it.

— Bernard Madoff (Richard Dreyfus)
Madoff (2015)

What is the world population? Approaching 8 billion? How many people are there in the United States? Maybe 350 million? How many people in your profession? If you sell real estate there are probably over 2 million people in the United States trying to do the same thing as you. That is 2 million! And there is only 1 of you.

Be exclusive. There is only one of you with your unique skills, experience, and passion.

CHALLENGE
How exclusive are you?

47
HIT HARD – HIT FAST –HIT OFTEN

Hit hard, hit fast, hit often.

> — Lt. General Lewis "Chesty" Puller
> The United States Marine Corps

The C19 Buzzwords are POWER, SPEED and PERSISTANCE. Hit hard, hit fast, hit often. A lot of people are using "pivot", but pivoting means absolutely nothing unless you pivot with power, speed, and persistence.

Think about what we have learned from our other strategies. First you must define who you are and know your "why". Second you must know what you are selling — how you plan to sell it — and your target clients. Third you must be innovative and agile. Fourth you must take massive action with power, speed, and persistence.

CHALLENGE
How hard do you hit, how hard, how often?

48
GIVE THEM WHAT THEY WANT

I want ten chocolate chip cookies. Medium chips. None too close to the outside.

— Howard Hughes (Leonardo DiCaprio)
The Aviator (2004)

This should be the simplest thing for you to do. When someone tells you <u>exactly</u> what they want then find a way to give it to them and determine if you can make money doing it.

"Ten chocolate chip cookies. Medium chips. None too close to the outside." Sounds easy. Why make it any more complicated. Find the cookies. Set a price. Done deal!

If you could do deals like that all day you would be in hog heaven. Find out exactly what people want as quickly as possible. Find what they want and out how much they are willing to pay.

49
FIND THEIR ACHILLES HEEL

Ah, but remember, my friends. Even Tramp has his Achilles heel.

— Boris
Lady and the Tramp (1955)

Achilles was the greatest of all Greek warriors and a hero of the Trojan War. His mother held him by one of his heels to make him invulnerable. The heel did not get covered by water and he was later killed by an arrow wound. That is the myth of the 'Achilles Heel.'

Know your vulnerabilities and especially know the vulnerabilities of your allies and opponents. Leverage off their fear and greed. There is nothing wring with it. It is not personal — it is just business.

CHALLENGE
What is your Achilles Heel

50
DON'T OVERSELL

You had me at hello.

— Dorothy Boyd (Renee Zellweger)
Jerry Maguire (1996)

The quicker you shut up the more successful you will be. Learn to listen. One of the biggest mistakes many rookie salespeople make is vomiting their enthusiasm all over everyone with whom they come in contact.

Ever been stuck with a life insurance salesperson or trapped in a timeshare presentation? How about a MLM meeting or encounter with a religious zealot?

In the Land of Desire everybody wants to buy — buy nobody wants to be sold. Stop selling! Curb your enthusiasm. Shut up. Listen. Do not make the mistake of talking yourself OUT of a deal. You had them at "Hello."

51
BE BRAVE

'You have plenty of courage, I am sure,' answered Oz. 'All you need is confidence in yourself. There is no living thing that is not afraid when it faces danger. The true courage is in facing danger when you are afraid, and that kind of courage you have in plenty.'

— L. Frank Baum
The Wonderful Wizard of Oz (1900)

What is courage? Unlike charisma which is a priceless gift from God courage can be acquired. How do we build courage in our lives? We build courage from pain, hurt and failing. The more me stumble the more we need courage to get back up. But courage comes from out guts and not our minds.

CHALLENGE
Was the Cowardly Lion cowardly?

_____
_____
_____

52
PRAY

I have been driven many times upon my knees by the overwhelming conviction that I had no where else to go. My own wisdom and that of all about me seemed insufficient for that day.

— Abraham Lincoln

Prayer is universal to all religions and beliefs. Sometime prayer is to ask for something — "God help me." And sometimes prayer is for gratitude — "All the praises and thanks be to Allah."

You may call it prayer or meditation or even something else. What is important is that you set some quiet time alone each day when you can think about who you are, what you are doing and, especially, why?

CHALLENGE
Where do you pray?

_____

_____

29
ZERO DARK THIRTY

For God and country. Geronimo.

— Patrick (Joel Edgerton)
Zero Dark Thirty (2012)

Forget about everything you <u>think</u> you know about economics. The C19 Economy is based on emotion rather than principles.

CHALLENGE
When are you going to jump?

Think about your road to millions as a covert operation — think black ops, think psyops, think *Apocalypse Now*.
— Martin Sheen as Captain Williard waiting for a mission in a Saigon hotel room:

"Saigon... Shit... I'm still only in Saigon... Every time I think I'm gonna wake up back in the jungle. When I was home after my first tour it was worse. I'd wake up and there'd be nothing. I hardly said a word to my wife until I said yes to a divorce. When I was here I wanted to be there. When I was there, all I could think of was getting back into the jungle. I'm here for a week now, waiting for a mission, getting softer. Every minute I stay in this room I get weaker. And every minute Charlie squats in the bush he gets stronger. Each time I look around the walls move in a little tighter..."

Some of us may relate Willard's reflection of the war:

"In a war there are many moments for compassion and tender action. There are many moments for ruthless action — what is often called ruthless — what may in many circumstances be only clarity, seeing clarity what there is to be done and doing it, directly, quickly, awake, looking at it.

30
FLIGHT OF THE PHOENIX

The phoenix hope, can wing her way through the desert skies and still defying fortune's spite, revive from ashes and rise.

— Miguel de Cervantes

We have choices. We can choose to follow or lead. We can choose to complain or change. And we can choose to leave or stay.

CHALLENGE
Do you prefer Hershey's Milk Chocolate or Hershey's Milk Chocolate with Almonds?

_____
_____
_____
_____
_____
_____
_____
_____
_____
_____

In Ancient Greece there was a mythical bird that lives several hundred years and then regenerates itself by being born out of the ashes of its predecessor. The phoenix is the ultimate symbol of strength, transformation, and renewal. Legend has it that even though the phoenix is immortal, like many other supernatural creatures, it's vulnerable to iron. Most superheroes and villains have their Achilles heel. We all know that Superman's weakness is kryptonite.

American's Achilles heel is not nuclear, biological, or chemical nor is it our dependence on China. It is not the pandemic nor is it the hysteria over racial injustice. The most immediate threat to America's society and economy is simply that we have lost confidence in ourselves and in our leaders. We are in a crisis of confidence — a crisis that has attacked nation's heart, soul, and spirit. And it did not start a few months ago nor even a few years ago. It started, perhaps, when the Bay of Pigs invasion failed. There were a few brief shining moments — like winning the Cuban Missile crisis and killing Osama bin Laden — but now many are ashamed to be Americans. We must move on like the **legendary phoenix.**

FIVE
PLAYBOOK

Donald Trump didn't just throw out the playbook, he set fire to it. And America loved it.

— Kyle Smith

Every game needs a Playbook and business is a game that needs a concise playbook more than any other.

CHALLENGE
Have you ever had a playbook?

_____
_____
_____
_____
_____
_____
_____
_____
_____
_____

YOUR
PLAYBOOK
is worth
MILLIONS OF
DOLLARS

PLAYBOOK

Many of history's fortunes have been made at the expense of others. It is believed that the lending of "food money" took place as early as 5000 BC when people needed "bridge loans" to live until their crops were ready to harvest or their livestock was ready to be slaughtered. And they charged as much interest as they could.

You have what may be a once in a lifetime opportunity to get super rich as global economies reopen. Capitalize on the information and inspiration in this guide and other tools and resources available to you. Create a **strategy, plan, playbook,** and **pitch deck**. And then make it happen like the **legendary phoenix**.

31
MADMEN, SHEEP & ZOMBIES

I call it the Madman Theory, Bob. I want the North Vietnamese to believe I've reached the point where I might do *anything* to stop the war. We'll just slip the word to them that, 'for God's sake, you know Nixon is obsessed about communism. We can't restrain him when he's angry—and he has his hand on the nuclear button.'

— H.R. Haldeman
Ends of Power (1978)

The pandemic did not create madmen, sheep, and zombies — but it has empowered them.

CHALLENGE
Make a list of zombie companies that will survive the pandemic.

Madmen, sheep and zombies will create the perfect storm for you to make your fortune. How much you make and how fast you make it will depend greatly on your ability to constantly appraise situations and capitalize on opportunities.

Madmen radicals will continue to promote mass hysteria and try to shame Americans into believing that we should apologize for everything our ancestors did or did not do. Many are paid agitators with their own agendas that have absolutely nothing with making America great again.

Sheep politicians will continue to kneel and cave into the demands of protestors — regardless of how ridiculous they might be. And, like Barack Obama did for two terms, Democrats as well as Republicans will keep apologizing for America's misdeeds at home and abroad since Leif Eriksson headed to the North American continent around A.D. 1000.

Zombie companies will be kept alive by the government if they continue to provide jobs. You can benefit if you determine which companies will survive and prosper in the long run.

32
Top Ten

Business opportunities are like buses, there's always another one coming.

— Richard Branson

There are no sure things, but these ten opportunities have the potential to benefit from the C19 Economy.

CHALLENGE
Make your own Top Ten list.

_____
_____
_____
_____
_____
_____
_____
_____
_____
_____
_____
_____

TOP
10
OPPORTUNITIES
for
YOUR
MONEY

1
CANNABIS

The biggest killer on the planet is stress, and I think that the best medicine is and always has been cannabis.

— Willie Nelson

This is number one because it is a hot topic. The cannabis industry has lovers and haters. Whichever you choose to be it is difficult to ignore the lure of the "green gold rush." Many people believe that the global cannabis industry will continue to grow exponentially.

As inviting as it may seem there are many risks and challenges involved so do your research and due diligence before you invest any of your green. The internet is full of information, but you should seek the help of someone who understands the industry. You can choose to invest in stocks or make direct investments.

2
CYBERSECURITY

Information is the oxygen of the modern age. It seeps through the walls topped by barbed wire, it wafts across the electrified borders.

— Ronald Reagan

The pandemic has been a catalyst in the growth of cyber world and the need for cyber security has gone crazy. The effects of cybercrime are massive and result in lost time and sometimes millions of dollars in cost. The Twitter Bitcoin scam cyber hack was just the beginning. The landscape for investing in cybersecurity looks entirely different than it did before the pandemic and will continue to expand.

You can invest in individual cybersecurity stocks or an exchange traded fund (ETF). There are lots of choices so do your homework and invest selectively.

3
BIOTECH

You know, the real problem, I think is the guy in the front seat, we got to get rid of him.

— Travis Kalanick
Cofounder of Uber

Investing in biotech and life sciences can be extremely rewarding and extremely risky. There are many companies to choose from and ETFs. Its critical that you know what a real biotech opportunity is and what is not.

You will need to define your individual risk tolerance and understand the specific risks or your biotech investments. Biotech investments have risks specific to their own industry. Some of these risks include regulatory setbacks, approval challenges, patent expirations, and loss of exclusivity, Study the industry and look for opportunities with the biggest potential without exceeding your risk tolerances.

4
REMOTE WORK

Technology now allows people to connect anytime, anywhere, to anyone in the world, from almost any device. This is dramatically changing the way people work, facilitating 24/7 collaboration with colleagues who are dispersed across time zones, countries, and continents.

— Michael Dell

You have probably experienced working at home sometime during the pandemic and may still be working from home.

Communication technology continues to shape the future of remote work. There are opportunities in remote work software, mobile work tools, and virtual reality conferencing. Companies like Zoom are obvious and there are other work from home (WFH) choices.

CHALLENGE
How many times did you use Zoom last month?

146

5
DIGITAL MARKETING

Many companies have forgotten that they sell to actual companies. Humans care about the entire experience, not just the marketing or sales or service. To really win in the modern age, you must solve for humans.

— Dharmesh Shah
HubSpot CTO and Co-founder

All you must do is to evaluate stocks like Facebook to convince yourself to consider investing in digital marketing. These days almost every pitch deck includes a digital marketing strategy.

The pandemic has provided digital marketing with the opportunity to further prove its adaptability and effectiveness.

CHALLENGE
Place a Facebook ad.

6
ECOMMERCE

It's hard to find things that won't sell online.

— Jeff Bezos

Amazon has completely disrupted retail. There is not enough room on this page to list the companies that have fallen as collateral damage to ecommerce.

Ecommerce has forever changed the way consumers shop and the way companies sell their products. Online purchases have gone viral during the pandemic and are continuing to grow daily.

You can invest in individual stocks or an ecommerce ETF. Or you can start or buy your own ecommerce company.

CHALLENGE
How much did you spend online last month?

_____

_____

_____

7
FINTECH

We're witnessing the creative destruction of financial services, rearranging itself around the consumer. Who does this in the most relevant, exciting way using data and digital, wins!

— Arvind Sankaran

Fintech is financial technology and refers to a broad range of tech applications. Two major components of fintech are payments and cryptocurrencies. This sector of financial services is dynamic, diversified, and multidimensional.

Investing in fintech can be speculative so do your research before settling on individual stocks or a fintech ETF. If you are tech savvy you might want to look for venture capital and start your own fintech company.

CHALLENGE
Make a list of fintech companies.

8
BLOCKCHAIN

Blockchain technology could change our world.

— Jack Ma

Blockchain is an extremely complex data technology which in simple terms is a structure that stores transactional records and ensures their security, transparency, and decentralization.

There are many ways to invest in blockchain technologies but the learning curve for investors is very steep.

Investing in a blockchain ETF may be best before moving into individual blockchain technology company stock.

CHALLENGE
Invest some time to fully understand how blockchain technology can benefit you.

150

9
DIGITAL AND CRYPTOCURRENCIES

The future of money is digital currency.

— Bill Gates

There is a difference between digital currencies and cryptocurrencies. Digital currencies are centralized and are controlled by people and computers regulating the transactions in the network

Cryptocurrencies are deregulated and are controlled by the community. Bitcoin is the digital currency that utilizes cryptocurrency to simplify and increase the speed of financial transactions with minimum government restrictions. There are many cryptocurrencies used to facilitate safe, secure, and secure financial transactions. There are various ways to invest including ETFs and through cryptocurrency exchanges. Bitcoin is best known — but caveat emptor.

10
5G

Unlike 4G and previous generations of technology, 5G is very different. In fact, it stands across the full network from mobile access to cloud core, from software-defined networking to all forms of backhaul, front haul, IP routing, fixed networks, software, and more.

— Rajeev Suri

5G is the new darling of Wall Street. There are many ways to invest in 5G including individual stocks, EFTs, and mutual funds.

5G technology is extremely complicated and very controversial. The sector moves quickly and what may be a good 5G investment today may not be the best 5G investment tomorrow.

This is Number 10 because it promises the most ROI but carries with it the most risk.

33
FORTUNE COOKIES

Prophesy is a good line of business, but it is full of risks.

— Mark Twain

Past performance is no guarantee of future results and especially during and after this pandemic we cannot assume that just because a stock or investment sector did well in the past that it will continue to do well.

Here are thirty-three factors that will influence the C19 Economy — submitted for your consideration.

CHALLENGE
Write your own pre-pandemic fortune cookie message.

_____
_____
_____
_____

33

Made in USA

FORTUNE

COOKIE

MESSAGES

with

Economic

Forecasts

1
DOOMSDAY

He is like a man living through the night before doomsday, with full knowledge that the sun will go nova in the morning, yet unable to enjoy the precious pleasures of this world because all his energy is devoted to wishing desperately that the foreseen end will not, after all, come to pass.

— Dean Koontz

A doomsday call (DD) is an option added to a bond which allows either the issuer or investor to redeem the bond early. We are not at doomsday and must believe that the world is not ending.

OPPORTUNITIES

_____
_____
_____
_____
_____
_____
_____

2
CHANGE

Progress is impossible without change, and those who cannot change their minds cannot change anything.

— George Bernard Shaw

If we have learned nothing else from this pandemic we have learned that the world can turn upside down overnight because it did.

Your ability to anticipate changes and take financial advantage of those changes will greatly impact your success in building and protecting wealth in the C19 Economy.

OPPORTUNITIES

_____
_____
_____
_____
_____
_____
_____
_____

3
COLD WAR II

It is in that spirit, the spirit of '76, that I ask you to rise and join me in a toast to Chairman Mao, to Premier Chou, to the people of our two countries, and to the hope of our children that peace and harmony can be the legacy of our generation to theirs.

— Richard Nixon
China — February 25, 1972

We were headed into a Cold War with China well before they decided to attack us with the deadly virus that caused the global pandemic. Now China is smack in the middle of the bullseye.

OPPORTUNITIES

_____
_____
_____
_____
_____
_____
_____

157

4
GOVERNMENT

The legitimate object of government, is to do for a community of people, whatever they need to have done, but can not do, at all, or can not, so well do, for themselves — in their separate, and individual capacities. In all that the people can individually do as well for themselves, government ought not to interfere.

— Abraham Lincoln

The role of local, state, and federal government is being redefined hourly and will be dramatically influenced by the presidential election on Tuesday, November 3, 2020. Our fate will be sealed on that date.

OPPORTUNITIES

_____
_____
_____
_____
_____
_____
_____

5
POLICY

Even people on the liberal side are starting to worry about going off a fiscal cliff.

— Clint Eastwood

The government has two tools available to try to fix the economy — monetary policy and fiscal policy.

Monetary stimulus is when a central bank adds money to the economy and/or makes it easier to access.

Fiscal stimulus is when a government increases its spending and hiring activity.

OPPORTUNITIES

_____
_____
_____
_____
_____
_____
_____
_____

6
INFRASTRUCTURE

You and I come by road or rail, but economists travel on infrastructure.

— Margaret Thatcher

To pull out of the Great Depression President Franklin Roosevelt put America to work with the Works Progress Administration (WPA) — an ambitious employment and infrastructure program.

Requirements for social distancing may have prevented a program like WPA but now that America is opening back up, we should aggressively start fixing our infrastructure.

OPPORTUNITIES

_____
_____
_____
_____
_____
_____
_____
_____

7
HEALTHCARE

The art of medicine consists of amusing the patient while nature cures the disease.

— Voltaire

With 10,000 Americans are turning 65 every day — along with the other major healthcare issues we had before the Chinese virus attacked the country — we need help.

We were ill prepared for this pandemic or any other national health crisis. We are still not ready for the graying of America or for the mental health collateral damage which the pandemic has caused. Let us fix our healthcare system as soon as we can.

OPPORTUNITIES

_____
_____
_____
_____
_____
_____
_____

8
GRAYING OF AMERICA

We don't stop playing because we grow old. We grow old because we stop playing.

— George Bernard Shaw

It is no fun getting old. And as much as baby boomers have endured and survived the American experience they did not sign up for this pandemic. The "senior market" is a goldmine for those who can relate.

The Graying of America impacts every other sector of the economy. Look for special opportunities in healthcare, leisure and entertainment, real estate, insurance, and wealth management.

OPPORTUNITIES

_____
_____
_____
_____
_____
_____
_____

162

9
GREAT WEALTH TRANSFER

The surest way to ruin a man who doesn't know how to handle money is to give him some.

— George Bernard Shaw

Seventy million Americans will be transferring seventy trillion dollars over the next twenty years. It is going to be like an elephant going through a boa constrictor. There will be tremendous opportunities for Innovators, Investors, Entrepreneurs, and Advisors who are talented, experienced, ethical, and especially empathetic.

OPPORTUNITIES

_____
_____
_____
_____
_____
_____
_____
_____
_____

10
LATINOS

In the end, the American dream is not a sprint, or even a marathon, but a relay. Our families don't always cross the finish line in the span of one generation. But each generation passes on to the next the fruits of their labor.

— Julian Castro

The Latino community in America controls tremendous wealth and will continue to grow exponentially. You do not have to be Latino or speak Spanish to participate in the Latino Wealth Experience, but you must understand Latino values and be passionate about helping.

OPPORTUNITIES

_____
_____
_____
_____
_____
_____
_____

11
LATIN AMERICA

To our sister republics south of our border, we offer a special pledge — to convert our good words into good deeds — in a new alliance for progress — to assist free men and free governments in casting off the chains of poverty.

— John F. Kennedy
Inaugural Address (1961)

Latin America is the new Asia. Do not be confused by President Trump's wall. Our arms are open to economic cooperation as evidenced by the new United States-Mexico-Canada Agreement (USMCA).

OPPORTUNITIES

_____
_____
_____
_____
_____
_____
_____
_____

12
ENTREPRENEURSHIP

You don't learn to walk by following rules. You learn by doing and falling over.

— Richard Branson

We are experiencing "Entrepreneurial Darwinism" —survival of the fittest. Many companies have already folded, zombie companies will eventually die, and new companies will soon replace them.

Go back through the Top Ten and these Thirty-Three Fortune Cookies and look for entrepreneurial opportunities.

OPPORTUNITIES

_____
_____
_____
_____
_____
_____
_____
_____

13
RESTAURANTS

It's easier to be faithful to a restaurant than it is to a woman.

— Federico Fellini

The restaurant industry was hit harder by the pandemic than perhaps any other sector of our economy. The list of fatalities is long and growing daily. One of the biggest challenges has been the ongoing confusion in the government regulation of restaurants.

The survivors will be some of the big chains. Small independent restaurants will keep dropping like flies. Stay away from this industry at all costs.

OPPORTUNITIES

_____
_____
_____
_____
_____
_____
_____

14
HOSPITALITY

Do what you do so well that they want to see it again and bring their friends.

— Walt Disney

Like the restaurant industry, the hospitality sector was hit hard, and it will be a long time before it fully recovers.

Major theme parks open and close and the 2021 Rose Parade has been cancelled. There is nothing but uncertainty in the hospitality sector. Business travel and conventions will have a tough time transitioning back from the virtual world. And it is anybody's guess about recreational travel.

OPPORTUNITIES

_____

_____

_____

_____

_____

_____

_____

15
TRAVEL

Live with no excuses and travel with no regrets."

— Oscar Wilde

The fallout in the travel sector has not even begin to register. Some carriers may never recover, and many planes will end up in the boneyard.

The costs to the airline industry far exceed loss of revenue from air traffic being down. It is amazing that carriers seem to have dodged the bullet and expect zombie airlines to cease operations as soon as government subsidies end. Stay away.

OPPORTUNITIES

_____
_____
_____
_____
_____
_____
_____

16
RETAIL

People don't buy what you do, they buy why you do it.

— Simon Sinek

Retail was a dying sector well before the pandemic hit America. Department stores are dinosaurs. Before the shutdown, many people went into retain stores to look and touch merchandise and then ordered online.

Ma and Pa retail is dead. Anybody and everybody who has a phone and a card and shipping address will continue to order online. That leaves people living in their cars or on the streets to shop locally.

OPPORTUNITIES

_____
_____
_____
_____
_____
_____
_____

17
HOUSING

If the economy grows, housing gets better, quicker.

— Jamie Dimon

The pandemic hit the housing market just when the housing market should have been starting to heat up for the spring and summer months. Faced with shutdowns, social distancing and economic uncertainty real estate activity continued at a slower pace as real estate professionals pivoted and adapted. Home prices are still strong across the nation with some buyers and sellers on hold. The biggest opportunities will be in income properties.

OPPORTUNITIES

_____
_____
_____
_____
_____
_____
_____

18
COMMERCIAL REAL ESTATE

A funny thing happens in real estate. When it comes back, it comes back like gangbusters.

— Barbara Corcoran

Before the pandemic, the commercial real estate industry was looking forward to a strong year of growth and development. Now it is a new game and the outlook is not good.

The longer the economy struggles to reopen the longer that economic uncertainty is prolonged. The commercial real estate market is positioned to suffer a delayed hit once the effect of failed businesses is known.

OPPORTUNITIES

_____

_____

_____

_____

_____

_____

19
FINANCIAL MARKETS

One of the most constant aspects of American life is change — and nowhere is it more evident than in our financial markets.

— Henry Paulson

Financial markets are at the center of the economy and must assume a leadership role in economic recovery. To achieve this, we must stay open minded and agile. We must be flexible and innovative and avoid knee jerk reactions. We must produce long-term solutions.

Technology will play the dominant role in the future of financial markets.

OPPORTUNITIES

_____
_____
_____
_____
_____
_____

20
TECHNOLOGY

If we continue to develop our technology without wisdom or prudence, our servant may prove to be our executioner.

— Omar N. Bradley

The C19 Economy is all about technology. Tech as an investment arena is virtually an unlimited theme — spanning all economic sectors from surgical robotics to ecommerce platforms.

Because short-term volatility is expected the play should be long-term as a we begin to have a real picture of corporate earnings. Invest in quality individual stocks, ETFs, and mutual funds.

OPPORTUNITIES

_____
_____
_____
_____
_____
_____

21
SMALL BUSINESS

I believe that economics is based on scarcity of markets. And it's possible to monetize your art without compromising the integrity of it for commerce.

— Nipsy Hussle

Pandemic disruptions continue to plague small businesses in the United States and around the world. Many businesses have been forced to close permanently. Others have become zombie companies holding on by a string while they wait for the economy to reopen. The biggest mistake that a small business owner can make is failure to face reality — holding on to the "dream" can be fatal.

OPPORTUNITIES

_____
_____
_____
_____
_____

22
M&E

Words are, of course, the most powerful drug used by mankind.

— Rudyard Kipling

According to PriceWaterhouseCoopers (PwC) the U.S. Media and Entertainment is the largest in the world. M&E has gotten a boost during the pandemic and is expected to grow at a rapid pace.

Trends to watch include digital media and video streaming. Emerging technology will enable M&E to continue to create and release innovative and exciting products and services to an ever-awaiting audience.

OPPORTUNITIES

_____

_____

_____

_____

_____

_____

_____

23
AGRICULTURE

Doomsday is near; die all, die merrily.

— William Shakespeare

We need food to live — there will always be a demand for agricultural products. Like others the agricultural sector's outlook is clouded by pandemic uncertainties.

The pandemic should have raised our level of awareness of the need for innovations in the global agricultural industry. As the world population grows the demand for food will grow accordingly. The biggest challenge will be to grow and produce healthy and nutritious foods that are affordable and widely available.

OPPORTUNITIES

_____
_____
_____
_____
_____

24
CURRENCY

As you know, in the latter part of 2008 and early 2009, the Federal Reserve took extraordinary steps to provide liquidity and support credit market functioning, including the establishment of a number of emergency lending facilities and the creation or extension of currency swap agreements with 14 central banks around the world.

— Ben Bernanke

The U.S. dollar is the dominant reserve currency in the world. When risk is high traders will buy U.S. treasuries increasing the demand for U.S. dollars. All currency trades are done in pairs unlike stocks.

OPPORTUNITIES

25
LIFE SCIENCES

The pricing of a pharmaceutical product is opaque and frustrating, especially for patients.

— Heather Bresch

This one is not as simple as it sounds. Medtech and biopharma companies face great opportunities and great challenges. Major drivers in the life sciences sector include intelligent drugs, wearables, gene therapy, personalized medicine, robotics, and gene editing.

Nutraceuticals (natural supplements) should explode in response to a new pandemic induced health kick.

OPPORTUNITIES

_____
_____
_____
_____
_____

26
MANUFACTURING

We've switched from a culture that was interested in manufacturing, economics, politics — trying to play a serious part in the world — to a culture that's really entertainment-based.

— Stephen King

Now Joe Biden is mimicking President Trump's mantra to bring manufacturing back to the United States.

Manufacturing will continue to be a global shell game — much like the game of laundering money. Creative companies find ways to avoid tariffs like manufacturing in China and shipping to Vietnam to label.

OPPORTUNITIES

_____

_____

_____

_____

_____

_____

27
CONSUMER GOODS

Consumption is the sole end and purpose of all production; and the interest of the producer ought to be attended to, only so far as it may be necessary for promoting that of the consumer.

— Adam Smith

Shifting consumer behavior during and after the pandemic are a given but difficult to predict. Geopolitical interdependency and complex supply chains are fluid factors that respond to— rather than drive — consumer demand. Reopening the economy will not guarantee recovery and many companies will continue to struggle for survival and profits. Watch healthy food product trends.

OPPORTUNITIES

_____
_____
_____
_____
_____

28
FOOD

Let's face it: so much of what we consume is not driven by knowledge but by basic craving and impulse. The process of what we eat starts in our heads. And no one is more in our heads than a food industry that spends billions of dollars in marketing its message in every means possible.

— Chuck Norris

Food is very important in the C19 Economy. Think natural, organic, gluten-free, dairy-free, vegan, free-range, pasture-raised, hormone-free, no trans-fat, no high-fructose corn syrup, plant based — healthy foods.

Invest in stocks or start a company!

OPPORTUNITIES

_____
_____
_____
_____
_____
_____

29
TRADE

Nationalism makes us poor because its Siamese twin, protectionism, will destroy the internal market and disrupt international trade.

— Franz Timmermans

You do not have to be an economist to understand what happened to world trade during the pandemic. But you may have to be a fortune teller to predict what world trade may look like once the shutdown is over.

World trade is playing a game of Chinese Checkers as the players try to figure how to arbitrage supply chains and deliver goods.

OPPORTUNITIES

_____
_____
_____
_____
_____
_____

30
TAXATION

You can't tax business. Business doesn't pay taxes. It collects them.

— Ronald Reagan

Where is all the money going to come from for PPP and government stimulus? The answer is simple and obvious. And that is only part of the cost of being attacked by China.

The magnitude of economic devastation is frightening. In addition to pumping money into the economy taxpayers will eventually pay for the costs caused by rioters. Over the next ten years the final pandemic tab could be as much as $20 trillion before inflation.

OPPORTUNITIES

31
ENERGY

I'd put my money on the sun and solar energy. What a source of power! I hope we don't have to wait until oil and coal run out before we tackle that.

— Thomas Edison

Energy is a hot topic and the operative word is "alternative." Innovators like Elon Musk will continue to pursue cleaner and more effective sources of energy to fuel the world.

In the meantime, you can trade crude oil futures on NYMEX or invest in energy company stocks, mutual funds, or ETFs.

Think "Back to the Future."

OPPORTUNITIES

185

32
ENVIRONMENT

Here is your country. Cherish these natural wonders, cherish the natural resources, cherish the history and romance as a sacred heritage, for your children and your children's children. Do not let selfish men or greedy interests skin your country of its beauty, its riches or its romance.

— Theodore Roosevelt

There is a financial tradeoff between the economy and the environment unless you are betting on the environment. Look for ways to capitalize on improving our environment and you will make a lot of money while protecting our future.

OPPORTUNITIES

_____
_____
_____
_____
_____
_____
_____

33
ROBOTICS AND AI

In 30 years, a robot will likely be on the cover of *Time* magazine as the best CEO. Machines will do what human beings are incapable of doing. Machines will partner and cooperate with humans rather than become mankind's biggest enemy.

— Jack Ma

Self-driving vehicles are already a reality and we are probably not that far away from flying around in Jetson's cars.

Billions will continue to be made in robotics and artificial intelligence at the cost of millions of jobs globally. The C19 Economy will be greatly impacted by this sector.

OPPORTUNITIES

_____
_____
_____
_____
_____
_____

The secret to wealth is simple: Find a way to do more for others than anyone else does. Become more valuable. Do more. Give more. Be more. Serve more.
— Tony Robbins

34
WEALTH SECRETS

Money is only a tool. It will take you wherever you wish, but it will not replace you as the driver.

— Ayn Rand

No two fortunes have been made in the same way. Everyone has his or her own secrets for making a fortune and they are not usually the ones offered by Tai Lopez or other wealth gurus on informercials.

CHALLENGE
Make a list of your own wealth secrets.

_____
_____
_____
_____
_____
_____
_____
_____
_____
_____
_____

13

SECRETS

for

MAKING A

FORTUNE

1
DARWINISM

It is not the strongest of the species that survives, nor the most intelligent that survives. It is the one that is the most adaptable to change.

— Charles Darwin

Survival of the fittest. That is what the C19 Economy is all about. People and companies are being turned into zombies subsidized by the government and as soon as that money disappears the zombies suffer.

CHALLENGE
Make a list of what you have done during the pandemic to strengthen your mind and body.

_____
_____
_____
_____
_____
_____
_____
_____
_____

2
THINK SUPER RICH

There are people who have money and people who are rich.

— Coco Chanel

"Think Big and Kick Ass: In Business and in Life" was published in 2007 by Donald Trump and coauthor Bill Zanker.

How much money do you need versus how much money do you want? Think BIG! Thinking big is easy — it is just a matter of putting more zeros after your numbers.

Start with a BIG idea and create a plan for making it happen.

CHALLENGE

What is the most money you have ever made in a year? What if you were stuck at that number for the rest of your life?

_____

_____

_____

_____

3
RULES OF 72 AND 69.3

The Rule of 72 is useful for determining how fast money will grow. Take the annual return for any investment, expressed as a percentage, and divide it by 72. The result is the number of years it will take place to double your money.

— Peter Lynch

This is a way to determine how long an investment will take to double given a fixed rate of return. By dividing 72 by the annual rate of return you can calculate roughly how many years it will take for your investment to duplicate itself. For example, divide 72 by a 6% annual rate of return and you will see that it will take approximately 6 years for your initial investment to double. For maximum accuracy — particularly for continuous compounding interest rate instruments — use 69.3.

4
NOMO FOMO

Before you try to keep up with the Jones, be sure they're not trying to keep up with you.

— Erma Bombeck

Do not believe everything you see on Facebook and Instagram pages. Those luxury cars may not even belong to your friends theirs and if you want one that bad you can lease a C-Class for $299 a month.

Read "The Millionaire Next Door" by Tom Stanley and you may change your mind about hanging out at Pelican Hill sipping Macallan while puffing on a Perfecto all financed by your credit card at 24% APR. Do not let FOMO get you into serious debt.

CHALLENGE
What is "generation Jones"?

_____

_____

_____

5
$1000 TO $1000000

A million dollars isn't what it used to be.

— Howard Hughes

Double $1,000 ten times and you will have $1,024,000. Here's how:

1	$1,000	x 2 = $2,000
2	$2,000	x 2 = $4,000
3	$4,000	x 2 = $8,000
4	$8,000	x 2 = $16,000
5	$16,000	x 2 = $32,000
6	$32,000	x 2 = $64,000
7	$64,000	x 2 = $128,000
8	$128,000	x 2 = $256,000
9	$256,000	x 2 = $512,000
10	$512,000	x 2 = $1,024,000

CHALLENGE
What are the odds of doubling your money ten times?

_____

_____

_____

6
PASSIVE INCOME

The key to financial freedom and great wealth is a person's ability or skill to convert earned income into passive income and/or portfolio income.

— Robert Kiyosaki

As soon as some people hear the term "passive income" the first thing that comes to mind is some get-rich-quick scheme or multi-level marketing "opportunity."

There are many sources of legitimate passive income including rental property or a business in which one does not actively participate (royalties, stock dividends, interest).Often passive income is confused with "multiple streams of income" which might include passive income as well as earned income.

CHALLENGE
Do you have passive income?

196

7
VALUE TIME

Remember that time is money.

— Benjamin Franklin

Time, like land, is a limited resource. The difference is that you can buy land, but you can never buy more time. You might be able to extend time, but you can never buy more.

If you do not value your time no one else will. Cherish every minute because you never know how much more time you have.

CHALLENGE
Calculate how much an hour of your time is worth and then calculate a minute of your time and then a second of your time. Are you surprised?

_____
_____
_____
_____
_____
_____
_____
_____

8
LEVERAGE OPM

The thing about using other people's money is that they're going to set the rules.

— Tyler Perry

Leveraging other people's money is not as easy as it sounds. Nothing comes without strings attached. Before you accept money from someone be sure that you completely understand what is expected of you.

Although most people believe you only need to control over 50% of the ownership of your company you should try to control 80%. Selling 20% or less of your company interest keeps you in position of safe control.

CHALLENGE
How much OPM can you raise by selling 20% of your company or idea and how can you do it?

_____

_____

_____

_____

_____

9
CASH FLOW IS KING

Never take your eyes off the cash flow because it's the lifeblood of business.

— Richard Branson

If you do not have cash flow you are going to eventually run out of money. Most savvy investors target both capital appreciation and cash flow. Cash flow is the life blood of any business and should be a priority.

CHALLENGE
When was the last time that you performed a personal or business cash flow analysis?

_____
_____
_____
_____
_____
_____
_____
_____
_____
_____
_____

10
VALUE OVER PRICE

Price is what you pay. Value is what you get.

— Warren Buffett

Whether you are buying or selling focus on value over price. If you are buying, consider what you are willing to pay and what you expect for the price you are willing to pay.

If you are selling create maximum value and do not sell yourself short. "Earning peoples' business" usually means little more than giving them the price they want or demand. Do not compromise yourself by selling price over value.

CHALLENGE
What added value do you bring to the table?

_____
_____
_____
_____
_____
_____

11
EXPERTS

It will not be enough to rely on experts. Ordinary citizens must become experts too. It will take public opinion on a wide scale to ensure that world leaders act.

— Mikhail Gorbachev

Most wealthy people do not prepare their own tax returns and the wealthiest rely on experts for tax, investment, and insurance advise.

CHALLENGE
Make a list of your experts.

_____
_____
_____
_____
_____
_____
_____
_____
_____
_____
_____
_____

12
IGNORE BULLSHIT

Bullshit is the glue that binds us as a nation.

— George Carlin

Vishen Lakhiani in "The Code for the Extraordinary Mind" talks about "Bullshit Rules (Brules)" that inhibit your ability to succeed.

Learn to ignore bullshit and bullshit rules that have the potential for getting you off of the market.

CHALLENGE
Make a list of the people you know who are only sudor y pedos.

_____

_____

_____

_____

_____

_____

_____

_____

13
LIMIT GOOGLING

The greatest challenge Internet users face is information overload.

— James Garner

The internet can be addicting and a big waste of your time. Limit your online time to activities that are required to achieve your immediate goals. Watching porn and playing games may not fall into that category.

CHALLENGE
Log your internet time for a week.

_____
_____
_____
_____
_____
_____
_____
_____
_____
_____
_____
_____
_____

In every crisis
there is opportunity.
Chinese Proverb

35

BELTS, ROADS, AND WALLS

The Belt and Road Initiative calls for exchanges between nations and civilizations for mutual understanding, rather than mutual resentment. It is important to remove, rather than erect, walls between each other, take dialogue as the golden rule and be good neighbors with each other.

— Xi Jinping
Cairo, Egypt — January 21, 2016

China's strategy is to lend its way into as many companies and countries as it can and then foreclose when the borrowers default.

CHALLENGE
Make a list of the reasons you think we should stay in bed with China.

_____

_____

_____

Do not — for even a minute — buy into China's fantasyland Belt and Road Initiative as being anything other than a greedy grab for global political and economic power. It is at the root of their long-term plan to control the world. Their true colors were exposed when they allowed their deadly China virus to quickly infect the world while they disseminated lies and fuzzy math to create foment hysteria.

China's financial tentacles reach far, wide, and deep. There are very few places where they have not invested or loaned money. While the world slept China tricked companies and countries into believing that doing business with them would be mutually beneficial. That could not be farther from the truth.

America should forget about Belts and Roads and probably even walls. While great walls protected the empire from savages, they shut off people from the world for centuries.
Let's focus on America — all of the Americas. On July 1, 2020, the free trade agreement between the United States of America, the United Mexican States and Canada (USMCA) entered into force replacing the NAFTA.

36
DEATH OF A SALESMAN

It's a measly manner of existence. To get
on that subway on the hot mornings in
summer. To devote your whole life to
keeping stock, or making phone calls, or
selling or buying. To suffer fifty weeks of
the year for a two week vacation, when all
you really desire is to be outdoors, with
your shirt off. And still-that's how you build
a future

— Arthur Miller
Death of a Salesman (1949)

---

*How long do you think it will be before
salespeople are entirely replaced by robots?*

CHALLENGE
What is the difference between a salesperson and
an order taker?

_____
_____
_____

I f you have the word **sales** anywhere in your title, on your business card or in your email address you should be scared — very scared. Most salespeople were dinosaurs long before the virus effectively shut down the world's economies.

Salespeople are going to be the biggest fatality of the pandemic. In order to survive in a sales career, you must quickly transform yourself like Franz Kafka's traveling salesman Gregor Samsa waking up to find he has been inexplicable transformed into a giant insect subsequently struggling to adjust to his new condition and circumstances (*The Metamorphosis* — 1915).

Do something before you wake up a ungeheures Ungeziefe which is German for "monstrous vermin." Arthur Miller's Willy Loman suffers from a distorted illusion of what is required to achieve the American dream.

Leverage technology and capitalize on what you have learned during the shutdown and forget about being a ungeheures and transform yourself into a **trusted advisor** instead. Survive salesperson Darwinism.

37

WE CAN BE

Can you say why America is the greatest country in the world? It's not the greatest country in the world. That's my answer…

— Will McAvoy (Jeff Daniels)
The Newsroom — S1E1 (2012)

Let us stop apologizing for our ancestors alleged improprieties and quit tearing down statues and renaming everything.

CHALLENGE
Make a list of everything you believe we need to save the American Dream.

_____
_____
_____
_____
_____
_____
_____
_____
_____
_____

In the opening episode of *The Newsroom* cable news anchor Will McAvoy, onstage at a university panel, responded to a question from a student: "… so when you ask what makes us the greatest country in the world, I don't know what the fuck you're talking about! Yosemite? It sure used to be… We stood up for what was right. We fought for moral reason. We passed laws, struck down laws, for moral reason. We waged wars on poverty, not on poor people. We sacrificed, we cared about our neighbors, we put our money where our mouths were and we never beat our chest. We built great, big things, made ungodly technological advances, explored the universe, cured diseases and we cultivated the world's greatest artists AND the world's greatest economy. We reached for the stars, acted like men. We aspired to intelligence; we didn't belittle it. It didn't make us feel inferior. We didn't identify ourselves by who we voted for in the last election and we didn't scare so easy. We were able to be all these things and do all these things because we were informed… by great men, men who were revered. First step in solving any problem is recognizing there is one. America is not the greatest country in the world anymore."

Donald Trump has **Make America Great Again** and now Joe Biden has **Keep America Great.**

38
ONCE AND FUTURE AMERICA

I don't have to tell you things are bad.
Everybody knows things are bad. It's a
depression. Everybody's out of work, or
scared of losing their job. The dollar buys
a nickel's worth, banks are going bust,
shopkeepers keep a gun under the
counter, punks are running wild in the
street, and there's nobody anywhere who
seems to know what to do, and there's no
end to it!

— Howard Beale (Peter Finch)
Network (1976)

*What we are experiencing now in many
ways is no worse than what Americans have
experienced over the history of our nation.*

CHALLENGE
What does it take to push you over the edge?

_____

_____

Wow. What a great celebration of 244 years of Independence. For many the experience was virtual — for others there were still the traditional parades, barbeques, fireworks, speeches, and flag-waving.

The American Revolution served as an inspiration for Latin America nations. Haiti, a French slave colony which shares an island with the Dominican Republic, was the first to follow the United States to independence. Creoles led by Simón Bolivar and other liberators followed with revolutions winning independence for the rest of Latin America.

Let's continue making (or keeping) America great by looking at our back pages, thinking about what we have learned, and using all of our resources to protect the most amazing economy in the history of the world.

Americans are badass — we have always been badass, and always will be badass. Now it is high time to be proud of who we are and get our economy moving again. Let us stop apologizing. Let us start kicking ass and taking names, America may not be perfect — but we are the Land of Dreams.

39
CRYSTAL BALL

I deal in facts, not forecasting the future. That crystal ball stuff. That doesn't work.

— Peter Lynch

Crystal balls are used in mentalism acts by stage magicians and the information gleaned from reading the crystal balls is used to predict life events surrounding important decisions including those related to business and finance.

CHALLENGE
If you had a reliable crystal ball what would you like to see inside?

_____
_____
_____
_____
_____
_____
_____

213

For months everyone is attempting to predict what will happen when — or if — we ever get out of this mess. Finally it's not about the underlying fundamentals of the economy or the markets. It's all about timing and determination.

We can make forecasts using "what ifs" but that is all a waste of time because there are so many unknown variables. Reopening the economy is no guarantee of recovery no more than past performance is a guarantee of future performance.

This is the time when we need to completely forget about the past and keep our energy entirely focused on the future.

It is dangerous when we start believing talking heads and financial gurus who either tell us how good or even how bad the economy was, is, or will be.

Forget about crystal balls and think about snow globes — you know the ones that have little scenes inside a glass ball with snowflakes that you shake up and let settle. We just need to stop shaking up the snow globes and let the snow settle.

40

BRASS BALLS

You want to know what it takes to sell real estate? It takes brass balls to sell real estate.

— Blake (Alec Baldwin)
Glengarry Glen Ross (1992)

This is the greatest time ever to be in the real estate industry. Historically more fortunes have been made in real estate during tough times than in good times.

CHALLENGE
Do you have what it takes to sell real estate?

_____
_____
_____
_____
_____
_____
_____
_____
_____

This chapter is for all of you who are in the real estate industry — or want to be. Many of you were not making money before the pandemic and have been hit particularly hard by the unexpected experience.

The real estate profession has faced major disruption for a long time and now has been pushed over the edge. Some people were able to pivot and find ways to keep going while others caved. Those who lacked talent and motivation found themselves at home seeking inspiration or direction from the growing number of zoom conferences. They sought a quick replacement for the broker previews, local board meetings, NAHREP or AAREA events.

This is the decisive moment. It is a simple decision. Turn in your badge or make a commitment to success. It is the perfect storm for you to make a fortune in real estate sales and investment. All the tools and resources are out there for you. Make the transition from salesperson to trusted advisor by getting your MLO endorsement, and life insurance license. Create a badass plan. You are the magic of selling real estate. Show it.

SIX
FINAL THOUGHTS

Money is neither good nor bad. Money simply multiplies who you are. If you're a good person, money multiplies that. If you're a bad person, money multiplies that.

— Vishen Lakhiani

Like Mark Twain's obituary published in the New York Journal (June 2, 1897) reports of the demise of the American economy have been grossly exaggerated.

CHALLENGE
Write your own obituary then fuggedaboutit.

_____
_____
_____
_____
_____
_____
_____
_____

The Fat Lady has been singing for a while, but the opera is still not over for America.

FINAL THOUGHTS

Arbitrage

Jimmy Grant: You think money's going to fix this?
Robert Miller: What else is there?

— Jimmy Grant (Nate Parker)
Robert Miller (Richard Gere)
Arbitrage (2012)

In economics and finance arbitrage is the simultaneous buying different investment vehicles like securities, commodities, and currencies — or derivatives — to take advantage of price differences between two or more markets.

CHALLENGE
What is options arbitrage?

_____
_____
_____
_____
_____
_____
_____
_____

At the end of the day life is one big game of arbitrage. And to succeed at life — like with arbitrage — you must know the difference between distinct types of opportunities and investments. Abraham Lincoln has often been quoted as saying" "How many legs does a dog have if you call his tail a leg? Four. Saying a tail is a leg doesn't make it a leg."

There are several arbitrage strategies that you can implement to consistently win the game of life: **Geographic, Time,** and **Trade.**

Geographic arbitrage takes advantage of differences in different locations and can be as simple as buying gas in one city because the price-per-gallon is less.

Time arbitrageurs can seek to reduce risk by simultaneously going long and short on future opportunities.

Trade arbitrage is based on the concept that everything is negotiable, and more value can sometimes be realized by trading goods and services.

Exploit differences in perceived value.

222

MILLIONAIRE

I'm not a bad person, I don't drink and I
   don't kill
I've got no evil habits and probably will
I don't sing like Elvis Presley, I can't dance
   Like Fred Astaire
But there's one thing in my favor, (what)
I'm a millionaire (that's beautiful)

> — Dr. Hook
> *The Millionaire* (1975)
> Kelis Rogers and Andre Benjamin

---

*Enjoy every mile and every hour of your
road to millions and remember that the
destination is not the millions of dollars but
all of the things you will be able to achieve.*

CHALLENGE
Watch *The Millionaire* on YouTube.

Millionaire is a concept that is overrated, overused, and grossly misunderstood. The most realistic and traditional meaning of "millionaire" is a person who had at least $1,000,000 in liquid and/or liquidable assets outside of their primary residence.

Many of you reading **C19 Economics** are already millionaires many times over and many more may become millionaires as the result of what you put into action after reading this guide.

The Millionaire is a black-and-white American tv series aired on CBS from 1955 – 1960. The anthology showed fictional multi-millionaire John Beresford Tipton gives people he does not know a check for $1 million in exchange for a signed agreement not to tell anyone how they received the money. It is interesting to learn how their lives changed.

There are countless modern-day stories of lottery winners who became overnight millionaires or multi-millionaires only to blow their money in a few years if not in just a manner of months. What would you do?

AMERICA

With a good conscience our only sure reward, with history the final judge of our deeds, let us go forth to lead the land we love, asking His blessing and His help, but knowing that here on earth God's work must truly be our own.

— John F. Kennedy
Inaugural Address (1961)

Do you believe that "God's work must truly be our own"?

CHALLENGE
How would you respond if someone were to ask you "Why is America the greatest country in the world?"

_____
_____
_____
_____
_____
_____
_____
_____

Imagine leaving the country of your birth heading for someplace called "America". Maybe you are alone or maybe you are traveling with some of your family members who were also fortunate enough to be with you. You cross the Atlantic in the crowded, dark, and filthy steerage of a dilapidated and leaky packet ship. You pray to God that you will arrive safely. Then one morning — hungry and feeling half-dead — you climb onto the deck and see the Statue of Liberty as your ship enters the harbor. Your heart stops.

We all ended up in America by various means and under different circumstances. Some walked over an ice bridge and others floated across the Rio Grande on inner tubes. Some came voluntarily as indentured servants — others were forced to come as slaves. Some travelled on steamships third class with all their possessions in carpetbags — others flew in first class on jumbo jets with designer luggage and fat bank accounts. Millions of people — each with their own story of *"Coming to America"*.

The real stories are the stories of what those people did when got here — the stories of what they did to make America great.

Keeping Up with The Parks
Henry Park

I don't care how much money you have son, just be a good person.

— Jung Sil Park

But I remember not having a lot of money twisted my soul. I mean when it came to making money, I was good at it. Maybe too good. I wanted to be like Gordon Gekko from the movie "Wall Street" growing up, not knowing who I became was not who my dad was proud of.

CONNECT WITH HENRY
hpark@secondarymg.com
Facebook.com/henry.park.940
Instagram.com/henryparkofficial
KeepingUpwiththeParks.com

People always ask me "Henry, can you show me how to make money?"
Shortly after the pandemic began, I began receiving an increased number of calls, emails, and texts from friends and associates asking for investment advice. I am a mortgage banker — not an investment advisor — but I have been investing successfully for a long-time.

To help people learn about making money and have fun doing it I started an investment group on Facebook — **Henry's Road to a Million** in May and it quickly grew to 1,000 members. And I have weekly Zoom conferences where we focus on investing in the real world.

I created the investment club because of a few reasons. One, I was tired of people talking shit on all rich people. You see money is a value proposition. You must create value if you want to make money. You see not all rich people are evil, but I thought maybe it's because most people don't know how to make money. So, I am going to teach you all the tricks I have learned from my buddies that worked in Wall Street and take it to Main Street. The goal is simple. I am going to take $1,000 and turn it into $1 million dollars within 3 years. Now for full disclosure, I'm not licensed as a stockbroker or anything like that and I am not asking you for money. In fact if you follow me you may lose money. I am merely showing you that it is possible. Anyone can be a millionaire, but it takes knowledge, time, homework, and discipline.

Each of us have different reasons for wanting to make money and each of us has our own investment styles. In order to understand my investment style, you need to learn a little about me. Although my story is on our family website: **KeepingUpwiththeParks.com** I am going to share a little of it here.

I was not born a "crazy rich Asian". You see growing up I had a father who was always working. Coming from Korea he struggled financially trying to learn a new language while providing for our family. My dad started as a gardener and joined the military so he could come to the United States. My mom was a travel agent working for Korea Airlines. They met in Guam and that's where I was born. We moved to Hawaii and then came to Los Angeles so you can see by 5 years old I had lived in three various places.

Growing up we always struggled financially. My mom became a waitress at a Japanese restaurant and my father worked as a cashier at a Shell gas station. All the Shell stations were required to stay open 24 hours a day 7 days a week. My dad was making minimum wage of $3.25 an hour and desperately need as many hours as possible to support our family. My dad slept overnight at the station in a little makeshift bed and I hardly ever saw him. It was at that point, there was a turning point in my life. I remembered hating life and wanted to see my dad, even hated the gas station for taking my dad away.

Since then I have made fortunes and lost fortunes and have made them back again. That's how life is. I invite you to read the rest of my story on our website. You will learn how losing my father to cancer dramatically changed how I look at money — and at life. I kept thinking about what my dad told me before he died: "I don't care about how much money you have son, just be a good person". I kept asking myself what he was talking about. And then one day I came home exhausted from work. My wife and I had worked until 1 AM and our nanny had put our kids to sleep. So, I just turned on the TV.

I was disappointed that my kids had to go to bed without seeing me and they were already asleep. Sitting there watching *Keeping up with the Kardashians,* hungry and tired, I just kept thinking and thinking. Why the hell am I coming home so late? What happened to me putting the kids to sleep like I promised I would do when I was a little boy who one day became a father. And why was I more concerned about what the Kardashians are doing in their lives when I have my own life to live. And so that was how the concept of KeepingUpwiththeParks was born.

I was going to be a different person. The one my dad was telling me to be on his deathbed. He gave me a gift. I couldn't change the past, but I can change the future. So now I've been re-born. Not the same person. I'm going to try to be the best husband and father to those 5 kiddos. Thank you, dad! I get it now! I love you with all my heart.

Before becoming a trader, I made money doing loans. I saved up $60,000 and put it towards a down payment on a condo in La Palma. It was a 2-bedroom condo that I bought for $160,000. My mortgage was $100,000 and my monthly payment was

$506. I was 21 years old at the time. I flipped that property just 3 years later and sold it for $225,000. Doubled my money. I guess you can say I got hooked. Since then I've been buying and flipping properties. I can't even count how many I've done but I would say on average 4-8 a year.

Most of the money I have made through the years has been in challenging times. The pandemic has created — and will continue to provide — tremendous opportunities to make lots and lots of money.

We have given you a lot of information in this book, but you need to make a plan and take action. Decide whether you are going to be an **Innovator**, **Investor**, **Entrepreneur**, or **Advisor**.

If you are a real estate salesperson or agent whose business has taken a big hit because of the pandemic, then this book should help you jump start your business again. Become a **360 Advisor** licensed in **Real Estate, Loans,** and **Life Insurance and Annuities.** If you are interested in supercharging your business to take full advantage of emerging economic and financial trends, we will sponsor you and help you get licensed and trained. Hit us up!

Wash Your Hands for Lunch
ROBERT MILLER

I love daddy…!
I remember when he was super happy.

— Ali Miller

In 1967 The Beatles sang about love in "All You Need Is Love" (by John Lennon and Paul McCartney) and love may be all we need to get through this pandemic.

There is nothing you can know that isn't known
Nothing you can see that isn't shown
There's nowhere you can be that isn't where
    you're meant to be
It's easy

CONNECT WITH ROBERT
RobertMillerNow@Gmail.com
Facebook.com/RobertMillerNow
LinkedIn.com/In/RobertMillerNow
Instagram.com/RobertMillerNow
Twitter.com/RobertMillerNow
RobertMillerNow.com

When our daughter was in kindergarten the happiest time of the day was lunchtime when the kids could run outside to the playground and play. Her teacher would yell "Wash your hands for lunch." and the fun began.

Not long before America's last economic meltdown leading to the Great Depression my life was out of balance. I was working sixteen or more hours a day and rarely saw my wife and our daughter Ali. One day Ali sent me this email:

I love daddy...! I remember when he was super happy.

You were so crazy and fun... remember yelling: "Wash you hands for lunch" going to San Diego and picking up the shells? Spending hundreds of dollars at Dave & Busters?

HAHA and the race cars... remember the race cars? We would race!

What about the times we went to Knott's Berry Farm to pick out geodes and you would get me those princess caps and we would pan for gold and go on the Dinosaur Ride?

234

Remember making messes at the restaurants with Tim & Patsy...? HAHA

That was so much fun, you were always so happy... and crazy, get crazy again... I like it when you are funny and crazy... like Dennis the Menace all grown up... that's how I remember you when I was little... like the really big kid... who was also really smart, always knew what to do, and took the best care of me no matter what!

I love you more than... what? The whole world! Do you remember when I first told you that after we left grandma and grandpa's? You were shocked... you said...

"really? More than the whole world?" HAHA And I said: "yes daddy, more than the WHOLE WORLD!" DADDY be crazy! DADDY ON THE LOOSE.

WASH YOUR HANDS FOR LUNCH!

As we publish *C19 Economics* America is five months into the pandemic nightmare. For a while now it has seemed like every day is just another day out of the movie *Ground Hog Day* (1993). I want some days like Phil (Bill Murray) talked about: "I was in the Virgin Islands once. I met a girl. We ate lobster and drink piña coladas. At sunset we made love like sea otters. THAT was a pretty good day. Why couldn't I get that day over and over...?"

My life has spanned eight decades that have taken me all over the world and I never imagined anything like what we have experienced and will probably continue to experience for months — if not years — as the direct and collateral results of the malicious and irresponsible actions of the PRC. It is ludicrous to when you consider how vulnerable the world was. It does not matter whether the virus originated in a laboratory or in a filthy "wet market" where exotic live animals and seafood were sold. It is difficult not to be resentful toward the Chinese government — but it's easy to wake up and make sure that nothing like this ever happens again. America was too busy buying everything in sight, partying, doing recreational drugs, posting selfies and pictures of other people's luxury cars on Facebook and Instagram, and doing everything we could to keep up with the Kardashians.

Many Americans might relate to these lyrics from *Against the Wind* (1980) by Bob Seger:

236

Guess I lost my way
There were oh-so many roads
I was living to run and running to live
Never worried about paying or even how much I
    owed
Moving eight miles a minute for months at a time
Breaking all of the rules that would bend
I began to find myself searching
Searching for shelter again and again

Some of us have taken advantage of the shutdown to reflect on our lives and — in some cases— reinvent ourselves. Others have allowed themselves to fall prey to the evil forces in America that would have us feel guilty for things that happened in America over which we had no effective control.

There are those who are advocating the complete "dismantling of America's political and economic system". The November 2020 election will, in many ways, determine the near-term and long-term future of America — and the world.

My strength during the pandemic has come from my belief in myself, in God, in the American system, and in the American people.

237

I have already shared my daughter Ali's email and she is an ongoing source of information, inspiration, and love.

The other Ali in my life — my wife — is the love of my life, my best friend, my partner, and my greatest source of strength. Every morning for many, many years she gives me the same speech that goes something like this:

"Work smart today — not hard. Remember who you are, and that God put you here on earth for a reason and gave you the ability to influence people. You change people's lives every day — you help make their dreams come true. Don't waste your time with sudor y pedos. Don't let anyone get you off the market. Stay BADASS. Trust your instincts. Be careful out there. I love you."

The title of this book is *C19 Economics: Your Guide to Personal and Business Finance.* Like me, you know that there are already too many financial guides on the market. And everyone is a "financial guru" — especially all of those newly licensed recruit drinking (and serving) the Kool-Aid at MLM meetings for all those get-rich-financial literacy clones whose 60 second speeches begin with "I help people... " and always include the words "financial literacy." By now you probably know that you need help with your finances but may not know where to get it.

The world of finance is quite different than it was when I began in financial services more than fifty-five years ago. If you do not believe me than watch a few episodes of *American Greed* and you will be asking yourself "how could those people be that stupid?" They were not just stupid — they were greedy. Markets are driven by FOMO — fear of missing out. Be bold, not greedy. *Audentes fortuna iuvat* means fortune favors the bold.

Within the pages of this book are everything you need to get started on your **Road to Millions** except what that little racehorse — Seabiscuit — had. Seabiscuit had **heart**. Heart is the x-factor that you combine with passion, desire, knowledge, experience, talent, and what "G's" call game to get the "cheese." Hopefully, you have heart and we have given you enough information and inspiration to "bring home the bacon". Do not be afraid to be a "Capitalist pig" but keep in mind that greed is not always good. And like they say on Wall Street: "**Bulls** make money, **bears** make money, **pigs** get slaughtered."

239

The Beatles discovered backmasking —
recording a message backwards onto a track
to leave a hidden message — on their *Rubber
Soul* in 1965. So here is my hidden message
that you do not have to play backwards but
you do have to flip over:

I am honored and grateful that you
have made it to the back of our book.
May your Road to Millions be
adventurous, exciting, and successful.
Hold on tight to your dreams.
Reach for the stars — all of them.
Think creatively.
Color outside the lines.
And wash your hands for lunch.

240

SEVEN
SECOND WIND

Half-wracked prejudice leaped forth, "rip
    down all hate," I screamed
Lies that life is black and white spoke
    from my skull, I dreamed
Romantic facts of musketeers
    foundationed deep, somehow
Ah, but I was so much older then,
    I'm younger than that now

— Bob Dylan
My Back Pages (1964)
Bob Dylan

This section is for the Baby Boomers with a special message: "Was it over when the Germans bombed Pearl Harbor?"

CHALLENGE
Listen to Oscar Issac's song "Never Had" from *10 Years* (2011).

241

What? Over? Did you say "over"? Nothing is over until we decide it is! Was it over when the Germans bombed Pearl Harbor? Hell no!

— Bluto (John Belushi)
Animal House (1978)

There are basically two types of baby boomers: those who live in the past and present and those who live in the present and future.

Veteran's hospitals and nursing homes are packed with baby boomers who are living in the past — and too many are barely living. They are the **"lost generation"** whose friends and partners have died and whose families have stuffed them somewhere to die. They were the hippies in Haight-Ashbury and the "Young Turks" on Wall Street. They rolled joints in the mud of Woodstock and fought in the rice paddies of Southeast Asia. Now they sit around and try to tell war stories to anyone who will listen or reminisce about their high school prom date. Many of these older Americans live with fear of dying from the virus if not something else very soon. It is sad to think about lives without hope —people who believe they have little reason to live.

And then there are the **"second wind"** baby boomers who have not given up on America — or on themselves. We will survive the pandemic and actively participate in taking the **C19 Economy** to the moon and beyond.

This section is for those **"second winders"** who believe in themselves and in America with the expectation that it will provide some information and inspiration to help them protect the wealth they have accumulated and show them ways they build more.

Whether you are retired or planning to retire the same seven strategies apply: **(1) You're your advisors; (2) Evaluate and protect assets; (3) Maximize ROI; (4) Create multiple streams of income; (5) Build wealth; (6) Value wellness; (7) Live with purpose.**

1 – List your advisors.

Make a list of your trusted advisors to include: Legal, Accounting/Tax. Wealth Management, Real Estate, and Insurance. Decide how much help you need and where you are going to get it. Make sure you have a family trust and it is current and has been properly funded. If you are planning to leave assets to someone it is wise to get them introduced to your advisors now and even think about beginning to transition to advisors that might better serve their needs. Invest the time and energy to evaluate your advisor relationships regarding costs and performance.

2 - Evaluate and protect assets.

Whether helped by a financial planning professional or doing it yourself — conduct a comprehensive analysis of your assets including investment accounts, real estate, and insurance. Make sure that you take full advantage of insurance products and annuities. Review risk, performance, and anticipated ROI vs. potential options.

3 - Maximize ROI.

Define objectives and risk tolerance and structure an agile portfolio which can easily be modified to allocate investment and real estate assets in anticipation of expected economic trends.

4 - Create multiple streams of income.

Hedge yourself by having income from as many sources as possible. If you have income from Social Security do not count on it — if you do someday you may be in trouble

5 – Build wealth.

It is never too late to begin to build wealth and there is always time to continue to grow the wealth you have accumulated — no matter how much or how little. The best way to build wealth is to invest in real estate or in a business.

6 – Value wellness.

Money without health is worthless. Wellness must be your number one priority. Invest time, money, and energy to extend your life but more importantly maximize your quality of life. Balance physical fitness (speed, strength, stamina, and flexibility) with health (body organs and functions). And do not forget about your brain and emotions.

7 – Live with purpose.

Why did God put you here on earth? You really "can't take it with you" — so think hard about what you are doing every day and the non-financial legacy you are going to leave. If you do not have a favorite charity or passion project, start one. Leave a legacy every day you are alive by freely sharing your experience and energy. Be proud of who you are and what you have done. Remember there is more time on the clock.

If you are a baby boomer you probably never imagined — in your wildest imagination — that you would be "sheltering in place" wearing masks and listening to Neil Diamond singing a version of *Sweet Caroline* with "hands washing hands" in the special lyrics.

Baby boomers have seen it all — from ducking under their desks during the Cold War to watching their heroes murdered on live television and having their friends come home from Vietnam in body bags.

Baby boomers still control a tremendous amount of political power and financial wealth in America. And they have the ability to continue to make priceless contributions to society.

The key to boomer longevity and prosperity is remaining agile and open minded — and paddling like hell before the waves roll over them.

Baby boomers must take control of their own finances and consider financial products and strategies like reverse mortgages and indexed annuities to build and protect wealth. But stay hypervigilant to avoid senior frauds.

246

EPILOGUE

The days of American passivity and naivety regarding the People's Republic of China are over.

— Robert O'Brien
United States National Security Advisor
June 24, 2020

The same week as Robert O'Brien gave the above quoted speech Newsweek's cover story was titled: "How America's Biggest Companies Made China Great Again."

FINAL CHALLENGE
What is China 2025?

_____
_____
_____
_____
_____
_____
_____
_____
_____
_____

The Land of Dreams has become **Land of Fear** and we have the right to be afraid — very afraid. Our lives are being attacked by the deadly China virus. Our economy is fighting for its life. And our American way of life is being threatened from within.

For America and Americas to survive and prosper we must immediately conquer the fear in our hearts and minds — and the fear in our institutions and on our streets.

Imagine yourself as a passenger on the *Titanic* and try to compare the experience with what you are experiencing now. Let us look at the **Timeline of the *Titanic's* Final Hours** written by Amy Tikkanen at *Encyclopaedia Britannica.* On the morning of April 14, 1912 Captain Edward J. Smith canceled a schedule lifeboat drill. After receiving several iceberg warnings, the captain changed course but maintained the ship's speed (5:50 PM). With most of the ship's passengers in their rooms for the evening the *Titanic* scraped its side along an iceberg. The ship's designer surveyed the damage and predicted that the *Titanic* had only two hours before sinking (11:40 PM).

The lifeboats were readied for launch but there was only room for 1,178 of the 2,000 passengers on board (12:00 AM). Thirty-five minutes after hitting the iceberg the captain ordered a distress signal to be sent out. Five minutes later another ship received the message and responded that it had changed course and was on the way to help but was more than three hours away (12:20 AM). The first lifeboat was was lowered carrying only 27 people even though it had room for 65 (12:45 PM). The only lifeboats remaining on the *Titanic* were three collapsible boats. With hundreds of people still on deck the captain released the crew saying, "it's every man for himself." The lights on the *Titanic* went off as the ship plunged into darkness (2:18 AM).

America is not a sinking ship and we are not going to go down while the orchestra plays on deck. But we must take control of our fear by educating ourselves because what we fear most is the uncertain and unknown. This is not as easy as it sounds because there is so much misinformation and propaganda out there. Try to make decisions based on what you know rather than what others are telling you — avoid speculation. Think long-term. Put things into perspective. Visualize success.

Let us look at what we are afraid of one at a time. First is the virus. Do what is under your control to protect yourself and your family by practicing social distancing, personal hygiene, and doing everything you can to stay strong and healthy. Do not let stress and anxiety compromise your wellness. Someday, hopefully sometime soon, the nightmare will be over. But let it be a wakeup call and a reminder to remain hypervigilant.

The second reason you may be afraid may be your personal finances. Being afraid is not going to help you improve your financial situation, but it may motivate you to take control of your finances. Everything you need to make money — lots of money — is here in this book. Do not allow fear to paralyze you.

You have control over your personal health and finances. But there are some other things that may appear out of your control that are creating fear and anxiety in your life. And those things require patience and understanding. Although you may believe that you cannot do much to change our economy or society that is not true. Do not give up. Become an influencer. Have an opinion and deliver it with conviction.

250

The November election will determine the fate of the American economy and the American way of life. Invest time to learn about the issues and make your vote count.

The real competition is not between two American presidential candidates. There are two campaigns. The first one is between Donald Trump and Xi Junping. It is the battle for the control of the American economy that the CCP began decades ago.

China began playing by its own rules around the time of the 2008 global financial crisis. After Xi Jinping took over, he made known China's intentions for controlling the world's economy with the **Made in China 2025** plan. His strategy is to buy or steal high technology components from the United Stated with the end game being for Chinese companies to dominate every major industry.

The United States has done everything it can to help Xi Jinping achieve his goal. As reported in the *Newsweek* cover story *How America's Biggest Companies Made China Great Again* "the role of big business in the current state of affairs can't be ignored." Few companies were able to ignore China's lure.

There are no easy answers. We might be trapped somewhere between heaven and hell. Lower costs from goods made in China are irresistible to consumers and businesses in the United States — so irresistible that we continue to ignore issues of world pollution and human rights in China. So irresistible that we have allowed PRC's blind and ruthless ambition to turn the world upside down and almost bring the global economy to its knees.

The issues extend far beyond who wins— the United States or China. China has never played fairly, and it is ridiculous for us to believe they ever will. Fair competition may exist in Fantasyland but not with the PRC. When the smoke clears we will discover that PRC's Belt and Road initiative is nothing more than a way of getting its hooks into developing countries who are not credit-worthy and loading them up with debt, refusing to renegotiate when they default on that debt, and then seizing the assets. Predatory lending at its fiercest.

The biggest threat to the United States is China's effort to disrupt our position as the world's foremost tech superpower.

PRC's obsession with achieving technological supremacy is no secret and is evidenced by their **Digital Silk** initiative and **Next Generation Artificial Intelligence Plan**. They have the technology and skills to create the highly sophisticated **Great Firewall of China (GFW)** and have the capacity to leverage 5G for corporate and military espionage.

While the CCP uses GFW for internet surveillance and censorship to control the Chinese people with an iron fist we bend over backwards to protect all of our citizens with the basic freedoms afforded by the Bill of Rights of the U.S. Constitution.

CCP has almost succeeded in their goal of destroying America from within by intentionally allowing their deadly virus to attack the world and then lying about it. If it sounds like a conspiracy theory or something out of a science-fiction movie it is not.

We remain under attack by the virus and many of us are angry, frustrated, and afraid. But we can no longer allow these pressures to pull our nation apart. The CCP has achieved their goal of destroying America from within and they see us rioting and

tearing down statues and monuments. Who knows how much Chinese money has gone to fund Antifa and Black Lives Matter?
Do not buy into Antifa, Black Lives Matter, and the cancel culture. We are in a propaganda war with PRC and all those powers wanting to see the rapid undoing of everything that has made America the most powerful nation in the world.

When you think about it much of the fear that we are now experiencing is related to financial matters. How many concerns about social injustice are economically based? What are the demonstrations, riots, and looting about if not money and power?

As much as some people would like to have you believe that socialism and communism are great, they are not. You must believe in a free market economy, capitalism, and democracy because you have read this book about building and protecting wealth

To make money, lots of money, you must understand how the economy works —all the players and moving parts. The C19 Economy, at this point in its cycle, is being driven Madmen, Sheep, and Zombie Companies.

Here is what we need to do as a nation. First, we must settle down emotionally and step back from all the hate and fear that has taken over our emotions. Americans are active and social creatures. This shutdown has us at a tipping point. And we do not need to keep having talking heads and corporate advertisers remind us that "we are all in this together," "Black Lives Matter," and that these are challenging or uncertain times.

Each of us must take a mandatory time out and think about our lives and what we want America to be. Someday we will look back and reflect on what we did in our lives and what we did not do. How can anybody be proud of destroying what others have given blood, sweat, and tears to build?

In spite of all of the communist and Antifa propaganda and all of the self-destructive behavior that many people are displaying now we know that America is the greatest place in the world — that is why we live here.

Let's remember what made America great and stop apologizing for it. We are strong and badass and we are going to survive this. We may not all be in this together, but we can be.

And make no mistake. We hold China fully responsible for concealing the virus and unleashing it upon the world. They could've stopped it. They should've stopped it. It would've been very easy to do at the source when it happened.

Donald Trump
White House Rose Garden
July 14, 2020

TOOLBOX

I don't believe in the kind of magic in my books. But I do believe something very magical can happen when you read a good book.

— J.K. Rowling

Tools in your toolbox, arrows in your quiver, or hacks— whatever you call them — have as many as you can always available.

CHALLENGE
Make a list of hacks that you have used.

_____
_____
_____
_____
_____
_____
_____
_____
_____
_____
_____
_____

FELIX THE CAT
had his little
Bag of Tricks
and you have your
Toolbox

TOOLBOX

60 Second Speech

Ideas alone are not scalable. Only when a idea is put into words that people can clearly understand can an idea inspire action.

— Simon Sinek

Some call it an elevator speech or 60 second pitch. If you have ever been to a leads group or networking event you have been asked to present one. Most of them sound the same because they begin with: "I help people..."

CHALLENGE
Watch Simon Sinek's *Start with Why* on YouTube.

_____
_____
_____
_____
_____
_____
_____
_____
_____
_____

Why do you do what you do? That's what you should be explaining in your **60 Second Speech**. Do not start out something like "I help people find their dream house... "

Smart people do not want to hear you vomit some canned pitch about how great your products are or how you will do anything to "earn their business" (which usually just means lowering the price).

Then what should you say in 60 short seconds? Passionately share your **WHY**. Something like this: "I believe that there is an optimal financial solution for every deal and I challenge myself to find it by thinking creatively, reaching for the stars, and coloring outside the lines to quickly close deals while providing world class experiences."

Be unique and keep your words at a sixth-grade level. And do not make it sound like a cheap sales pitch. Be confident. Do not sound condescending or patronizing.

Perfect your speech by recording videos on your phone in whatever languages you speak fluently. Then add it to texts and emails.

262

PERSONAL PLAN

A goal without a plan is just a wish.

— Antoine de Saint-Exupéry

Create a dynamic digital plan in a Word file so that you continually modify it and easily share it.

CHALLENGE
Squeeze your plan down to a one-page document.

This is a personal plan — not a business plan. You will create your business plan in the next sections: **Game Plan** and **Playbook**. Think about this **Plan** as a personal flight plan like the ones that pilots prepare and file prior to taking off — indicating the plane's planned route. Flight plans follow a standard format detailing the flight path and include departure and arrival points, estimated flight time, alternate airports in case of bad weather, whether the flight is visual or instrument, name of pilot and crew, passenger list and details about the aircraft (fuel, cargo).

Invest time and effort into creating your own "flight plan." Keep it simple. Your challenge will not be what to put in; your challenge will be what to leave out. Your plan should be dynamic and flexible.

Keep in mind that this plan is for your own use. It should describe your vision, your "why" and how and when you plan to achieve your dreams. Include **who, what, where, when, how,** and **why**.

After creating your plan in a Word document memorize it and save it on a flash drive.

264

GAME PLAN

You don't get abs like these eating peanut butter patties.

— Joe Kingman (Dwayne Johnson)
The Game Plan (2007)

We all have dreams and we should hold on tight to our dreams — all of them. But without a game plan a dream remains nothing more than a dream. And many dreams slowly morph into sudor y pedos before completely disappearing.

A plan without action is useless and action without a plan can be ineffective. You need both to be effective.

CHALLENGE
How has the pandemic affected your game plan?

_____
_____
_____
_____
_____
_____

A Game Plan is more than a business plan. Your game plan is where you visualize your dreams and then record your strategy for achieving them.

Although many of us do not remember his name most of us have heard the story about the POW who spent seven years in a prison cell mentally playing golf. It is the story of combat pilot Major James Nesmeth who was shot down over North Vietnam. Locked in solitary confinement his daily game plan was to play a round of golf in his mind. Every day he imagined getting dressed in his favorite golf clothes, driving to his country club, and playing a round of golf. Because he was playing the game in his head every game was perfect. Not long after returning home to the United States he went to his club and played a real game of golf — his best game ever. Although he had lost a lot of weight and was playing with a body that had deteriorated while in prison he played his best game ever because his mind was sharp and he followed his rehearsed game plan.

Be creative. Visualize the perfect dream like Major Nesmeth visualized the perfect game of golf. Think big — very **BIG**.

266

PLAYBOOK

The Democrats, the left has this 30-year playbook of how to destroy conservatives by simply exposing the horrible, the mean-spirited, insensitive things they say, but that isn't going to work on Trump the way it works on conservatives, for a whole host of reasons.

— Rush Limbaugh

Constructing your Game Plan was the hard part — making your Playbook is the fun part. Keep it simple and easy to read. Use a lot of graphics and colors. Primarily your playbook should be compelling, complete, organized, and logical. Make it special.

CHALLENGE
Create a name for your Playbook.

_____
_____
_____
_____
_____

Your **Playbook** should be your most valuable tool. Creating an effective playbook requires a commitment to excellence. Remember that is more than a business plan — it is a play-by-play guide to everything you included in your **Game Plan**.

Here is a unique concept for Playbook. Create an account at wix.com and pick a name for your Playbook. You can select a template and build a website to manage your game plan. Your Playbook will be hosted online and you can make it password protected.

Make your Playbook dynamic and fun. It should be a living document that can be modified and improved at any time. Be sure to include **company overview, products and services, ideal customer profile, marketing, sales methodology, compensation**, and **resources**.

Your Playbook is a work-in-progress that you will update and modify, as necessary. Putting your Playbook online will make it accessible to your entire team at any time. If you do not want to build a website for your Playbook you can use a group Google doc.

268

PITCH DECK

Investors don't look at pitch decks for very long — just an average of 3 minutes and 44 seconds.

— Tech Crunch
Techcrunch.com

Combine the power of emotions and the magic of storytelling with amazing graphics to create powerful visual presentation. You do not have to be entirely transparent, but you should avoid lying, exaggerating and everything that might be perceived as being deceptive or misleading.

CHALLENGE

Make a list of the different pitch decks you need.

_____
_____
_____
_____
_____
_____
_____
_____

The majority of what we take away from most presentations is **visual**. Your **Pitch Deck** is a public document designed for a multitude of reasons including financing and promoting your idea or company.

Ideally you will have several versions of your pitch deck — each with their own specific purpose. You should have one pitch deck for investors and another for presenting your company in conferences or at meetings.

There are several pitch deck templates online that you can reference in order to get some ideas for creating your own. Do not be a copycat. The key to a compelling pitch deck is originality.

When writing your pitch deck remember that you can make the most impact through the power of emotions and the magic of storytelling.

The number of slides and average reading time for each version of your pitch deck will depend on the target audience. Investors have shorter attention spans and want to get to the heart of your pitch quickly.

VIDEOS

I'm a little bit naked, but that's okay.

— Lady Gaga

You're a movie star! Why not? Everyone else is. The key to creating killer videos is quality. Remember that your video directly reflects who you are. And once t has been published you can never take it back so do not share anything that you don't want online forever. Be super creative. Go crazy and have fun. And stay focused on why you are shooting the video in the first place.

CHALLENGE
Right now, make a 60 second video on your computer or phone — make it fun.

Videos are the best way to tell your story and your story is the best way to raise capital and promote your idea or business.

There is an art to making videos and the skills you need can be learned only one way — through trial and error. The more video experience you get the better your videos will be. And the best videos and not the most perfect ones. The best videos are the ones that are candid and real.

Here are a few tips for creating impactful and captivating videos:

1. Use the back camera on your phone.
2. Use a solid-colored background.
3. Make sure there is plenty of light.
4. Use a good microphone for best audio.
5. Develop a strong camera presence.
6. Experiment with different angles.
7. Edit with a app like iMovie.
8. Have a script before you begin.
9. Aggressively promote your videos.

Making professional videos will take time but you should create lot of videos and post them on Facebook, YouTube, and Instagram.

RESOURCES

The most precious resource for business people is not their time. It's their energy. Manage it well.

— Robin Sharma

A Google search of the word "wealth" returns 469 million results in 49 seconds. There are more resources out there than you can ever use. Here are a few resources that may help you build and secure tremendous wealth as an Innovator, Investor, Entrepreneur, or Advisor.

CHALLENGE
Make a list of your favorite resources.

_____
_____
_____
_____
_____
_____
_____
_____
_____

RICHARD BRANSON
Business magnate, investor and author.
Screw Business as Usual and others.

JEFFREY GITOMER
Author, speaker and trainer.
Little Red Book of Selling,
Little Black Book of Connections
and many other great business books.
gitomer.com

VISHEN LAKHIANI
Entrepreneur, author, speaker, and activist.
The Code of the Extraordinary Mind
and *The Buddha and the Badass*.
vishen.com

TONY ROBBINS
Life and business strategist.
tonyrobbins.com

SIMON SINEK
Author, speaker, and influencer.
Start with Why and other inspiring books.
simonsinek.com

OLIVER STONE
Director, producer, and writer.
Apocalypse Now and
Untold History of the United States.

274

Acknowledgements

Nothing is original. Steal from anywhere that resonates with inspiration or fuels your imagination. Devour old films, new films, music, books, paintings, photographs, poems, dreams, random conversations, architecture, bridges, street signs, trees, clouds, bodies of water, light and shadows. Select only things to steal from that speak directly to your soul. If you do this, your work (and theft) will be authentic. Authenticity is invaluable; originality is nonexistent. And don't bother concealing your thievery—celebrate it if you feel like it. In any case, always remember what Jean-Luc Godard said: "It's not where you take things from—it's where you take them to."

— Jim Jarmusch

Thanks to all the influencers who share their thoughts and beliefs. Always have an opinion and deliver it with conviction.

ACKNOWLEDGEMENTS

Nothing is original. From the moment we are conceived we are influenced by sights and sounds. Our brains are the most amazing computers in the world. We store everything somewhere and our thoughts and beliefs are a dynamic compilation of our ongoing experiences.

The people, songs, and movies cited within the pages of this book all influenced in some way the book's contents. Sometimes there is no better way to say something better than how it has already been said.

A basic challenge when authoring a book is deciding what to leave in and what to leave out. Using Google helped in researching quotes and song lyrics. Hopefully, credit has been given where credit is due.

The main content does not come from studying economics but from closing and losing thousands of financial deals over many decades.

The perspective and opinions expressed herein are solely those of the authors so there's not really anyone to acknowledge except maybe all those lost deals.

276

ACKNOWLEDGEMENTS

Don McLean
William Barr
Bruce Springsteen
Franz Kafka
Donald J. Trump
Paul Simon
Neil Diamond
Camelot
Oliver Stone
Winston Churchill
Nassim Nicholas Taleb
Isoroku Yamamoto
Barry, Robin, and Maurice Gibb
Guns N' Roses
Vincent Bugliosi
George Orwell
Tim Rice
Thomas J. Stanley
Wall Street
John Templeton
John Stuart Mill
Jack Benny
Richard Branson
Bobby McFerrin
Steve Jobs
S. Balaram
Thomas Edison
Benjamin Graham
Henry Kravis
Warren Buffett
Buckminster Fuller
M.I.A.
Plato
Rounders

277

ACKNOWLEDGEMENTS

Pablo Picasso
Cocktail
Donnie Brasco
Vince Lombardi
Felix the Cat
Ruthless People
Arthur Miller
Chinatown
Paul Newman
Jeff Bezos
Steve Martin
Mad Men
Shel Silverstein
Walt Disney
Toby Jones
Coming to America
William R. Leach
John Lennon and Paul McCartney
Shrek
LL Cool J
Lewis Carroll
Pretty Woman
Boiler Room
Raymond Chandler
Back to School
Robert Greene
Oscar Wilde
The Godfather
Gordon Ramsey
Joel Osteen
Mark Zuckerberg
Wayne Gretzky
Alice in Wonderland
Caddyshack

278

ACKNOWLEDGEMENTS

J.M. Barrie
Glengarry Glen Ross
The Front
Mambo Kings
Madoff
Lewis "Chesty" Puller
The Aviator
Lady and the Tramp
Jerry Maguire
L. Frank Baum
Abraham Lincoln
Zero Dark Thirty
Miguel de Cervantes
Kyle Smith
H.R. Haldeman
Willie Nelson
Ronald Reagan
Travis Kalanick
Michael Dell
Darmesh Shah
Arvind Sankaran
Jack Ma
Bill Gates
Rajeev Suri
Mark Twain
Dean Koontz
George Bernard Shaw
Richard Nixon
Clint Eastwood
Margaret Thatcher
Voltaire
Julian Castro
John F. Kennedy
Federico Fellini

279

ACKNOWLEDGEMENTS

Simon Sinek
Jamie Dimon
Barbara Corcoran
Henry Paulson
Omar N. Bradley
Nipsy Hussle
Rudyard Kipling
William Shakespeare
Ben Bernanke
Mark Twain
Dean Koontz
Ben Bernanke
Heather Bresch
Stephen King
Adam Smith
Chuck Norris
Franz Timmermans
Theodore Roosevelt
Ayn Rand
Charles Darwin
Coco Chanel
Peter Lynch
Erma Bombeck
Howard Hughes
Robert Kiyosaki
Benjamin Franklin
Tyler Perry
Richard Branson
Warren Buffett
Chris Skinner
Michael Gorbachev
George Carlin
James Garner
Xi Jinping

280

ACKNOWLEDGEMENTS

Arthur Miller
The Newsroom
Network
Vishen Lakhiani
Arbitrage
Kelis Rogers and Andre Benjamin
Ali Miller
Bob Seger
Bob Dylan
Animal House
Oscar Issacs
Robert O'Brien
Newsweek
J.K. Rowling
Antoine de Saint-Exupéry
The Game Plan
Rush Limbaugh
TechCrunch
Lady Gaga
Jim Jarmusch
Curtis Mayfield

Cold, cold eyes upon me they stare
People all around me and they're all in fear
They don't seem to want me but they won't admit
I must be some kind of creature up here having fits

From my party house, I'm afraid to come outside
Although I'm filled with love I'm afraid they'll hurt my pride
So I play the part I feel they want of me
And I pull the shades so I won't see them seein' me

Havin' hard times in this crazy town
Havin' hard times, there's no love to be found
Havin' hard times in this crazy town
Havin' hard times, there's no love to be found

From my party house I feel like meetin' others
Familiar faces, creed and race, a brother

But to my surprise I find a man corrupt
Although he be my brother, he wants to hold me up

Havin' hard times in this crazy town
Havin' hard times, there's no love to be found
Havin' hard times in this crazy town
Havin' hard times, there's no love to be found

In this crazy town
Havin' hard times, there's no love to be found
Havin' hard times, in this crazy town
Havin' hard times, there's no love to be found

— Baby Huey
Hard Times (1971)
Curtis Mayfield

LATINO
INVESTORS
ENTREPRENEURS
& ADVISORS

OFFICIAL 2021 GUIDE

ROBERT MILLER
HENRY PARK

FOREWORD BY
MR. ABC - AMADO HERNANDEZ

ROBERT MILLER
HENRY PARK

FADING DREAMS
AND
RISING FEARS
AMERICA ON THE EDGE

THE MAGIC
OF
SELLING

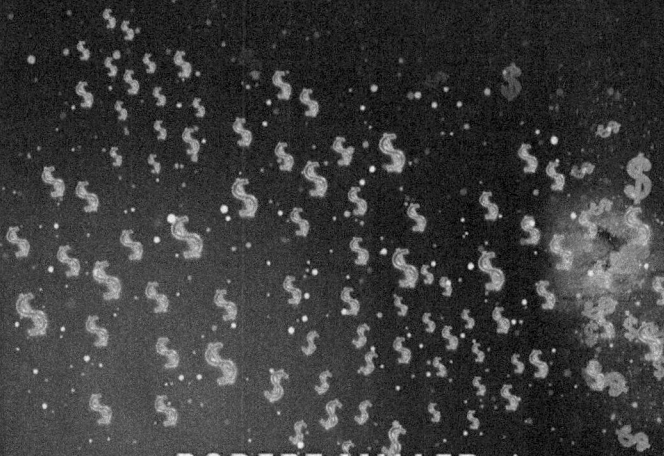

ROBERT MILLER

RAINMAKING

ROBERT MILLER

SECOND WIND

WIND

THE MAGIC OF MAKING
YOUR LIFE GREAT AGAIN

ROBERT MILLER

HENRY PARK'S

ROAD TO A MILLION

HENRY PARK

HENRY PARK'S
ROAD TO A
MILLION

COLLECTOR'S EDITION

HENRY PARK

If you would like to be contacted by a

Trusted Advisor

or are interested in learning about

Career Opportunities

in

Real Estate, Lending, Insurance, and Consulting

Send an email to:

Advisrz@Advisrz.com

GLOBAL ADVISORS NETWORK

www.ingramcontent.com/pod-product-compliance
Lightning Source LLC
Chambersburg PA
CBHW060326200326
41519CB00011BA/1854